The Insider's Guide

To Planning The

Perfect Wedding

TO MEGAN,

I USED THIS BOOK TO PLAN MY OWN WEDDING (OCT 21, 2000), TO UNCLE DAVE. I HOPE YOU AND MICHAEL WILL FIND SOME USEFUL INFORMATION IN HERE. JUST HAVE FUN & DON'T SWEAT THE SMALL STUFF.

Mary J. Carter

WE ARE ALL HERE TO HELP YOU WITH ANYTHING YOU NEED.

SO EXCITED FOR THE BOTH OF YOU! ALL MY LOVE ALWAYS!

AUNT DONNA :)

FONT & CENTER PRESS
P.O. Box 95
Weston, Massachusetts 02193

Published by
Font & Center Press
P.O. Box 95
Weston, Massachusetts 02193

Artwork and cover illustration by Donna Stackhouse
Book design by Becky Allen Mixter
Author's photograph © 1993 Gene Ritvo

Illustrations reprinted courtesy of Dover Publications from *1800 Woodcuts by
Thomas Bewick and His School,* edited by Blanche Cirker, *Humorous Victorian
Spot Illustrations,* edited by Carol Belanger Grafton, *Food and Drink, A Pictorial
Archive from Nineteenth-Century Sources,* selected by Jim Harter, *Men, A Pictorial
Archive from Nineteenth-Century Sources,* selected by Jim Harter, and *Victorian
Spot Illustrations, Alphabets & Ornaments,* selected by Carol Belanger Grafton

Printed in the United States of America on recycled paper
First printing March 1994
2   3   4   5   6   —   98   97   96   95   94

Library of Congress Cataloging-in-Publication Data

Carter, Mary J., 1957–
        The insider's guide to planning the perfect wedding / Mary J.
Carter.
            p.   cm.
        Includes index.
        ISBN 1-883280-03-6 : $13.95
        1. Weddings.   I. Title.
BJ2051.C36   1993
395' .22--dc20
                                                                93-48268
                                                                CIP

This book is lovingly dedicated
to Terry
for the push
and to Ilene
for the wings to fly with.
With heartfelt gratitude to all the brides
I've laughed and cried with over the years.
You've taught me more than you'll ever know.

Author's Introduction

Many of us dream of grandiose weddings. We imagine making our vows in vine-clad cathedrals and entertaining our guests afterwards in a mansion that overlooks the sea. But reality often paints a bleaker picture for those of us living in suburbia. Our churches are simple, our backyards small, and the only mansions in town (if indeed there are any) either have people living in them or are occupied by historical societies with strong aversions to 150 wedding guests frolicking about the grounds.

But don't despair! Even if the only function facility within 20 miles of your church offers a cut-and-dried package plan, you can have the wedding reception of your dreams. And this is the handbook that tells you how.

For 17 years, I worked as a wedding consultant for a large hotel chain. As director of my department, I chose to personally host many of the wedding banquets we booked, partly because I became terribly attached to every bride I worked with. But more importantly, I learned so much by carrying each consultation through to the reception itself. I saw what worked and what didn't. And I'm grateful for all the knowledge that has come my way.

Now I'm bringing that knowledge to you. By becoming aware of your options, you will be able to go to any function facility fully prepared to have things go your way, and not just be told by some sales rep "how things are done." Not only that, I am crossing the line of my profession to advise you of all the ins and outs the average function facility doesn't want you to know. With this guidebook, you will have before you all the questions you will need to ask, as well as an array of creative ideas that will make your reception unique and as individual as you are.

The best of everything to you, future bride! And may your most special day be blessed with perfection.

Table of Contents

Chapter 3

Are These Package Plan Prices Fair?

Chapter 4

The Final Selection:
Which Reception Site Is Best For You?

Chapter 5

Alternative Reception Sites

Chapter 6

Showing Your True Creative Self

Chapter 13

Getting It All Together

Chapter 14

With Many Thanks

Chapter 15

When You Have to Cancel

Chapter 16

And in Closing . . .

Index

Chapter 1

Getting Started

Setting Your Wedding Budget

When a Dollar Saved Is Approximately Fourteen Thousand Nine Hundred and Ninety-Nine Less Than You Need

Now we women are not going to kid ourselves. From the moment our hearts knew we were with the men of our dreams, we secretly began to plan our weddings. We've thumbed through endless bridal magazines for that oh-so-perfect dress, and we've envisioned just which of our childhood friends and family would stand witness to our oh-so-perfect day. But now the truth of it all is staring you in the face. These dreams are going to cost money.

Who Pays For What?

Back in the days of *Father Knows Best*, father paid for almost every aspect of his darling daughter's wedding. But in these modern and somewhat economically strained times, wedding costs are now very often covered by three "teams" — you and your fiancé, your parents, and your fiancé's parents. For the sake of tradition, here is what is normally covered and by whom:

The Bride's Family

* Announcements and invitations
* The wedding gown and related accessories
* Trousseau
* The bridesmaids' luncheon or social party
* Photography
* Rentals and related fees for the church or ceremony site
* Clergy's fees
* Musicians and vocalists at the ceremony
* Flowers for the ceremony and reception sites
* Flowers for the bridesmaids and boutonnieres for the ushers
* Corsages for the mothers and grandmothers
* Limousine transportation
* All aspects of the reception: food, beverages, flowers, entertainment, rentals, gratuities, and all related costs
* The groom's wedding ring
* Gifts for the bridesmaids
* Hotel accommodations for out-of-town bridesmaids

The Groom's Family

* The rehearsal dinner
* The marriage license
* The bride's engagement and wedding ring
* The bride's flowers
* Gifts for the best man and ushers
* Hotel accommodations for out-of-town groomsmen
* Wedding night suite for the bride and groom
* The honeymoon

Once again, this is just a guideline. You will know best what pertains to your particular family situation. Are either your parents or your fiancé's parents divorced? Are either of you devoted to a stepparent? Traditionally, your natural parents act as hosts on your wedding day, but only you and your fiancé can dictate what is easiest in your case and will make everyone — or almost everyone — happy.

My personal suggestion is that you and your fiancé should privately discuss the type of wedding you both would like to have. Then bring these ideas to your parents. Anyone you allow to make a major

In the early days of Puritan America, a young man needed permission from the girl's parents just to court her. And if he made "a motion of marriage" without formal parental consent, he faced imprisonment, monetary fine, or the whipping post. Most every young lady of the day was given a wedding dowry. This generally referred to a sum of money paid either all at once or annually, although a share of crops was sometimes instituted. This dowry was openly discussed and often debated between father and future son-in-law. And a newlywed husband rarely hesitated to sue when it seemed that the dowry was not coming through as planned!

Consider Miss Hannah Hull of Boston. She received as her dowry her weight in silver coin — a very tidy sum for colonial times. Imagine all the candies, cakes, and sweets her suitors tempted her with!

financial contribution should have some say in the festivities. So now is the time to either learn compromise or do without your parents' money for your wedding. The choice is yours.

The first step in knowing how much your wedding will cost involves estimating how many guests will be invited.

When each set of parents makes a financial contribution equal to yours, the total number of allotted guests should be divided by three. In this way, any team wishing to invite more than their allotted number of guests would simply pay the additional costs. This is by far the fairest method. **But for now, each team should make a complete list of everyone they would like to invite.** You and your fiancé, your parents, and his parents should all sit down and independently make a list. Don't leave out your favorite cousin Cathy just because you think your parents are going to list her. And if a friend or relative is single and unattached, write "and guest" next to that person's name. For one, things can change. And two, every wedding guest list grows larger as the day draws near. It's better to know now what that full list is going to cost you.

Next, alphabetize your lists and compare. Once you have deleted any duplications, you will have a good idea of the maximum number of people to quote when pricing out your reception costs.

Don't worry if the number on one list greatly outweighs the others. These things have a tendency of working themselves out in the long run.

Deciding When to Get Married

We all have specific reasons for selecting the day on which we wish to be wed. But there are some guidelines and restrictions to consider, such as:

The Day

Simply stated, allow yourself enough time to carry out the plans of your dreams. A few short weeks is not enough time to find a designer gown, and some banquet facilities are booked as much as three years in advance. It is terribly important to know that everyone you want in the bridal party will be available. Need time to save money? Factor that in, too. Yes, choose your wedding date wisely, but don't afford yourself too much spare time. Idle brides tend to get cranky and end up wishing the whole thing was over with. The average engagement these days seems to be between one year and a year and a half.

The Weather

If you live in a section of the country where snowstorms are a given, you may wish to avoid a winter wedding. Oh, there is a lot to be said for gentle scenic snowfalls and beautiful bridesmaids all decked out in red velvet. But a reception that faces a blizzard cancellation can be a gigantic headache. And summer weddings present problems all of their own as well. Most churches are not air-conditioned, making July and August rather unpopular months. And summer is when many of your intended guests may have already made travel plans.

Honeymoon Plans

It is important to arrange time off with your employer for your honeymoon in order to avoid unnecessary disappointment later. Also, the desired location of your honeymoon may have a lot to do with the time of the year you plan to wed. Remember that island resorts are typically unbearably hot and humid in the summer months. If the Caribbean is your romantic destination, the fall is the best time to go.

Your Menstrual Cycle

Some women run like clockwork, while others are affected by the least little thing. And often the hectic and nerve-racking pace of planning a wedding can throw even the most methodical of cycles into a tailspin. Now, your period is the last thing you want to bring along with you on your honeymoon. So just do your best to count out the weeks. If you've been irregular (it's a good idea to keep a chart) then simply take the average of your last four months.

Holidays — Religious, Personal, and Otherwise

Christian practices typically do not allow marriage ceremonies to occur during Lent, but if such timing is imperative to you, do check with your church.

Make positively sure that among your most important family members there is not another special occasion already planned on the day you wish to wed, such as a silver anniversary or a very special birthday party. And as for calendar holidays, it is not advisable to marry around the Thanksgiving or Christmas holidays for the simple reason that many of your guests will wish to be with their own families at these times. However, if a holiday wedding is your one true desire, be sure to notify everyone on the guest list as soon as possible. If you wait to send out your invitations in the standard four to eight weeks, you may be bitterly disappointed.

The Place and the Time

The Ceremony

Unless you plan to be married by a Justice of the Peace, the location of your nuptials should be decided upon with your spiritual needs in mind. Many of you have been brought up in a certain house of worship and this is often an easy choice. But when a conflict of religion exists between you and your fiancé, you must carefully work out all the details to meet both of your needs and desires. Try not to let parents pressure you! How you plan to raise your children may assist you in your decision-making. Don't hesitate to make an appointment with the clergy of your fiancé's house of worship (or he with yours, depending on what the case may be). You will want to understand everything about the faith you and/or your children will be entering.

When approaching the ceremony site of your choice, have an alternative date in mind, just in case. And when choosing the time of day, if your house of worship is flexible, keep in mind that most function facilities prefer to book two wedding receptions per room on Saturdays. Typically, the first arrival would have the room until 4:30 or 5 p.m. If the facility has a sizable working staff, the evening reception might be given an arrival as early as 6 p.m., although 6:30–7 p.m. is more the norm.

In other words, don't plan your ceremony in such a way that you and your guests have two hours to kill before cocktails.

Obtain from your clergy all requirements and restrictions, in writing if you can. Know what documents of proof you will need, when you will need them, and if premarital counsel is required. And be sure to determine to some degree how long your service will be, so you may quote a fairly accurate arrival time when seeking your reception site.

The Reception

Once the ceremony site has been set, get out the yellow pages and contact every banquet facility within easy or acceptable driving distance of your church. Ask family or friends if they have ever attended a social function at any of these places. Make note of their likes and dislikes, but always keep in mind that the final judgment rests with you. Besides, if someone makes a negative comment about a particular banquet facility, you can always contact your local Better Business Bureau to inquire if any formal complaints have been lodged against that facility.

When phoning the hotel, restaurant, or function facility, ask to speak with the banquet sales office. Furnish your requested wedding date, arrival time, and estimated number of guests, and ask that all menus and package plans (when available) be mailed to you. Do not hesitate to call the most expensive place in town, or even the one you vowed you'd never have your reception at, because the menus and planners may provide you with ideas you never thought of, as well as handy price comparisons. When calling, you need not commit to anything, or provide your phone number. Just reply politely that you will look over the brochures and get back to them if you're interested. And if any particular place claims to be booked for your requested day or dates, ask for the material anyway, explaining that you are still in the planning stages.

Then sit back and wait. But you shouldn't wait too long. The best banquet sales representatives will get the information out to you that very same day if they know anything about the value of your business!

What Is a Wedding Package Plan?

Any hotel, restaurant, or banquet facility that offers an all-inclusive package plan is doing its best to attract your business by providing all the aspects of a perfect wedding reception for today's busy working woman.

Prices vary greatly as package plans may include any or all of the following:

* Use of a **private banquet room** for no less than **five hours**
* Specially coordinated **linens**
* Elegant **silver service** for the **head table**
* Services of a **maitre d'** or **reception room hostess**
* Selection of a **full-course meal**
* An array of **hors d'oeuvres** for your **cocktail hour**
* **Bartender service**
* **Open bar** for your **cocktail hour**
* Choice of Chablis, rosé, Burgundy, or champagne **wedding toast**

* **Guest table** and **head table centerpieces**
* **Corsages, boutonnieres,** and **bridal bouquets**
* **Deluxe limousine service**
* **Professional photography and/or videography**
* **Live band** or **DJ**
* **Wedding cake**
* **Overnight accommodations for the bride and groom**
* **Invitations, guest book and pen, toast glasses, cake knife, cake napkins, embossed matchbooks,** or **place cards**
* All applicable **taxes** and **gratuities**

The facilities that offer these plans have spent extensive time and energy interviewing bakeries and bands, florists and photographers, limo drivers, linen companies, etc. They have tirelessly checked references, seen samples, and judged for quality all those things that you would have to do on your own. In other words, the legwork has already been done for you. And if you're short on spare time in your life, a package plan may just be the thing for you.

Other pluses for the wedding package plan are as follows:

* You will not have to write out endless deposit checks all over town. Your banquet facility will request an initial blanket deposit which covers everything.

* The services are guaranteed. You won't have to worry if the limo is going to show up, or if the cake arrived on time. The responsibility rests with the function facility alone.

And what of the minuses? Well, you are paying for the privilege of having all these aspects of your wedding worked out for you for sometimes as little as a few hundred dollars; sometimes as much as a thousand. If you are interested in a package plan reception, you will want to see the guide on page 47 where I'll help you figure out your costs, based on the plan you like best.

Can you get a credit on any service the plan offers that you would prefer to provide yourself? Generally, yes. But credits would only pertain to the services the facility does not offer on its own. For example, you won't receive a refund on head table candelabras. But more than likely, you can get a discount should you wish to provide your own band instead of the one they provide.

A word of warning, however. The credit price you'll be quoted may sound terribly low. And this will cause you to question the quality of service provided. Well, now's the time to explain how it all works.

I'll use music as an example. The band or DJ who is fortunate enough to appeal to both the banquet facility and to you will very often start off with a Friday night wedding then leave their equipment in place and return for two receptions on Saturday and one on Sunday. The same general idea applies to the lucky florist, photographer, and limousine company: a minimum of five weddings per weekend. In turn, these choice selected service industries or individuals most often provide discounted rates to the banquet facility in exchange for the windfall of business. This is essentially why the credit rebates offered to you on package plan services may seem somewhat low should you elect not to use them. And of course, there are always those facilities who are just not going to give you the full refund. Oh, that band may cost them $1,200, but you'll find yourself ending up with only $600 back if you don't want to use them. Unfortunately, such a practice is more commonplace than you may think.

My personal advice to you is simple. Judge each facility by what it offers. I believe in package plans for busy women, as long as the prices reflect the quality offered. I do not, however, recommend package plans for women who have the ability, time, and patience to place their own personal signature on every aspect of their reception. A package plan then becomes just a waste of your money.

Read on. Now let me show you ways to make your wedding reception truly yours!

One bad dream that most brides share is the "function factory nightmare." You walk into the ladies' room at your reception facility only to encounter another bride attired in exactly the same gown you're wearing.

You want to feel special and be the only bride for a million miles on your wedding day. But the larger the function facility, the more chance you'll have of running into another wedding booked at the same time as yours. So what can you do?

If you're positively enthralled with a banquet facility that accommodates more than one wedding at a time, find out just how close your room is to the next reception. Be sure to investigate the soundproofing to make sure that the bands or DJs won't conflict. As long as your party is given undivided attention from a properly manned staff, you will be able to shut out the rest of the world and celebrate your wedding entirely by yourselves.

Still skeptical about sharing your special day? Then head for the suburbs. Most smaller hotels — 250 sleeping rooms or less — have only one ballroom; thus, only one wedding reception at a time. Whatever the case, establish your needs early. You'll have plenty to dream about as it is!

Investigating Possible Reception Sites

Arranging the First Meeting

Once you have received all your brochures, read them carefully over and over again, making note of each one's pluses and minuses as you see them in print. Now if it seems to you that no one out there is offering anything unique, don't feel frustrated. Remember that these facilities are sending out suggested menus and guidelines, and you can very often adapt these plans to suit your particular style.

Next, call each facility that appeals to you and book an appointment with a banquet sales representative, making sure that your wedding date or alternative dates are still available.

If at all possible, arrange your appointment for a time when you can view the room or rooms in question. Understand, however, that on any given afternoon or evening during the business week you are most likely going to see the room set for a corporate classroom or meeting. Your appointment may take up to two hours. With that in mind, try not to book more than one or two appointments for the same day unless time restrictions apply. You may feel too overwhelmed to differentiate one place from another after a full day of banquet hall "shopping."

This will be the first step in selecting your perfect reception site and a full guide to answering your initial questions follows. The second step involves seeing the banquet room fully set for a wedding (when time permits). The third step will address all your "personal touch" problems before you hand over that ever-binding deposit.

Just one important note, however. Don't let the date slip through your fingers by dilly-dallying over your decision. A good sales rep will offer to contact you if someone else is interested in putting down a deposit for the same date you want. But don't leave something this important to chance.

Your First Appointment

You will want to begin your wedding appointment by repeating your requested wedding date and time to your banquet sales representative just to be assured that it's still available.

Your sales rep will want to know your anticipated number of guests. Report a range of from 25 less to 25 more than your actual list total. (For example, if your list shows 200 names, tell the sales rep you expect 175–225 guests.) This information will determine which banquet room or rooms best suit your needs.

If at all possible, see the banquet room(s) right away. If you hate it, this saves valuable time for both you and the sales rep. Keep in mind, however, that if the room has just been vacated by a business meeting, you must overlook the scattered chairs and the empty coffee cups. Concentrate on the rug, the walls, and the lighting instead. Is everything clean? Look at the linen on the tables. Is it fresh and crisp, or unduly soiled and wrinkled? Remember that the same company who supplies their everyday linen will most likely be supplying your wedding day tablecloths and napkins.

Will the room decor clash with your choice of bridal colors? Does the tone of the room fit in with your sense of celebration? For example, is the atmosphere too formal? Or not formal enough? Is the wallpaper peeling or puckered, or is the paint faded or soiled? Are there any inoperative light fixtures? Remember that lightbulbs and linen can be changed, but walls and rugs obviously cannot. However, be sure to ask if the facility plans to make any renovations prior to your wedding date! This can factor a great deal in your decision making.

While you are standing in the banquet room, ask the following questions:

1. **Where would the head table be placed?** Make sure, of course, that you know how many you wish to have seated at your head table. Generally, it would be the bridal party itself with parents seated at the tables of prominence (numbers one and two). The arrangement is entirely

up to you. It might be good for your peace of mind to find out the maximum number of people they can accommodate in any given area of the room.

2. **Would all guest tables be set in view of the head table?** Keep in mind that a full capacity seating may involve a few specific seats being out of a perfect sight line. This may or may not be of much importance to you. After all, you will be seated only while eating. And as these tables are typically the farthest ones away, you are not likely to place an important friend or family member there.

3. **Where would the band or DJ be placed?** Is it in clear view of the head table? How many guest tables are in close proximity to this area? You will need to place your "younger" friends near the music. Older folks don't appreciate being seated right next to blaring speakers, etc.

4. **Where and how big is the dance floor?** If the room doesn't already have an inlaid dance floor, ask for the dimensions. Now, if you can't visualize 9' x 12' (and most of us can't) ask the sales rep to "walk out" the size in the location where it will be placed. Repeat your number of guests and make sure that the dimensions you are being quoted will still hold for that size group. And what if you have a few more guests than anticipated? Would the room at full capacity mean that the dance floor would have to be cut down in size? Dancing is important! Once things get going at your reception, most everyone will want to dance. And an overflowing dance floor is frustrating.

5. **Where does the bar go?** With luck, it can be set within your function room. It is extremely ill-advised to allow a bar, particularly an open bar, to be set up in a public hallway! Your wedding guests will not be wearing special name tags, and no bartender is going to be able to distinguish your guests from the ones down the hall who, after discovering theirs is a cash bar, figure yours is a better deal. Can people really be this dishonest? Unfortunately, yes. I have personally witnessed this

happening as a guest at someone's wedding. Do not, I repeat, do not let this happen to you!

6. **Where will pictures be taken?** View this room. Do the draperies and/or walls complement your intended bridal colors? This is very important, as most of your formal wedding portraits will be taken in this room. Is the room large enough to accommodate your full bridal party in a single picture? Of course, if this particular room does not suit your needs, you should definitely ask if another room might be available.

After viewing the rooms, return to the office before discussing meals, music, etc. You will be less distracted and, once seated, you are better able to take notes.

Take out your package plan and/or menus and be sure to cover all of the following questions in this, your initial meeting.

Guarantee of Room

What happens if your actual number of guests falls below the estimated count? Can your room assignment possibly be changed without your knowledge or approval?

On the other hand, **what happens if that number exceeds the estimated count?** How many will this room actually hold?

Note that in either case you will want to keep in close contact with your banquet sales representative. If it appears that a great number of your guests cannot attend, you may wish to consider a smaller room, if one is available. But also keep in mind that the banquet staff is accustomed to dealing with such problems, and is very adept at making 150 look very comfortable in a room that seats 200. So, don't panic.

Is this function area accessible to handicapped guests?

Guarantee of Hours

If you plan a **Saturday afternoon reception**, you will most likely be confined to a 5 p.m. departure time or perhaps even earlier, unless you pay an exorbitant rental to stay on through the evening. Do ask, if keeping the party going at the function hall is important to you, but financially it may not seem worthwhile.

Evening receptions usually have more leeway for staying later. Ask your sales rep how many hours are allocated for nighttime weddings. (You should be quoted five hours.) If this brings your reception to a halt at say 11 p.m., ask if any arrangements can be made to keep the hall until the licensed hour for bar closing. If a rental figure is quoted, ask under what circumstances that amount can be waived or at least decreased — for example, if your bar, the purchase of additional food, or a combination of both reach a certain dollar amount. All the same, it is often easier to continue the party where you are than move it to someone's house — usually your parents'— for more food and drink. The band may be hired to play additional hours, or a DJ can be brought in for a change of pace.

Food

Package plans typically have set menus featuring the most popular entrees. This does not mean you have to stick by them, but keep in mind these basic rules:

Specialty meals, such as *lobster fra diablo* and *veal calabrese* are not easily prepared for large groups of people, nor do they "sit" well during any minor time delay. Besides, not everyone likes them.

If you have a package plan offering various chicken, turkey, and beef entrees and none of these options pleases you, ask to see a regular banquet dinner menu if you don't already have one. Then, judging by your anticipated number of guests, inquire as to which items can easily be prepared for a group your size. Discuss suggested courses that complement each offering, but don't fret over fruit cups and vegetables at this time. All of this will figure in later.

Many brides I have worked with have wondered if they could offer their guests **a choice of chicken or beef**. This is more than gracious on your part. And, if I may, I would like to point out the pitfalls of such a practice:

Let's say your anticipated guest count is 200. Now, no banquet facility is going to specially order and prepare 200 chicken and 200 beef meals just to be ready for whatever happens. Not unless you pay for it, of course.

Therefore, to offer this choice, you, the bride, will be responsible for gathering the **exact** count per entree. This may sound easily arranged by sending a little "return form" with your invitations. But people will be people. Some of them will forget to fill it out, or they'll simply assume that they're supposed to bring the slip of paper with them to the reception. This means that **you** will be making endless phone calls during that precious last week before the wedding — a time, I may point out, that you will have far more important things to think about.

You, for example, may be responsible for supplying each guest with a "marker" card that indicates to the server which entree is to be served (e.g., blue cards for chicken and red cards for beef). This involves a great deal of participation on everyone's part. Your guests must remember to bring the cards and present them at dinner time. And then, there will always be guests who will tell you how they want their beef cooked or, worse yet, change their minds at the reception. In short, such operations rarely run smoothly, and always take valuable time away from your reception! After all, would you rather dance and have a good time, or while away the night figuring out who gets what on which plate?

A possible solution is to offer a **buffet**. By doing so, you have alleviated all the headaches your family is creating by insisting that you do "something other than chicken" at your wedding.

There are pros and cons, of course. The "pro" is simple. All your guests get to eat what they want, and how much they want. The "cons" are as follows:

* You may not want to go through a buffet line and risk damage to your lovely wedding gown. This is understandable. A head waiter or waitress should or could be instructed to serve you.

* Many of your guests may not wish to risk their clothing by going through a buffet line. This is true, to some degree. Just don't insist on a black-tie wedding. Or, indicate on your invitation that a "Buffet Reception" immediately follows. This little message puts the responsibility of attire strictly with the guest.

* Elderly people shouldn't have to stand in line for a buffet. True, once again — especially for any guest in a wheelchair. In such a case, speak with that person's escort or family member in advance, and ask that they see to his or her needs.

* Buffets almost always cost more than a single entree selection.

But all in all, the ease of a buffet may be worth it. Fine establishments typically set a beautifully decorated buffet table, making the entire effect far more dazzling and appealing to your guests.

If you are considering a buffet, make sure that the addition of a buffet table and adequate standing area will not crowd the banquet room with your anticipated guest count.

The Test Is in the Trying

Ask if it is possible to try any or all of the entrees you might be interested in having. (Of course, if you are leaning towards buffet, it will be rather difficult to try each and every item.) The best way to go about this is as follows:

1. Have a meeting with all "the powers that be" i.e., your fiancé and one or both sets of parents — whoever is equally hosting your reception, and narrow down your menu choices as much as possible. Decide who is going with you on your "taste-testing mission" and what are they going to eat. For obvious reasons, you all shouldn't order the same thing!

2. Try to arrange the taste-testing for a time in which you can actually see the banquet room set for a wedding, if time permits (meaning that you're not waiting three months for the next wedding!). If it's the middle of winter and the next wedding doesn't occur until April, try to see the room set for a formal dinner — even a Christmas party! Anything that will give you a proper idea of how your wedding setup may look.

3. Make sure the food you are trying will be prepared by the banquet chef. Many facilities have more than one kitchen, resulting in the need for two or more culinary chefs. It is pointless to try the food someone else has cooked.

4. Be prepared to pay for the food you eat. Some places will offer to charge you very little, or make some adjustment if and when you choose their facility for your reception. But in any case, sample the food if it is important to you. And it should be.

Hors d'Oeuvres, Deli Trays, and Sweet Tables

Ask for these menus if you don't have them already. But you needn't fuss with details at this time. Your need for hors d'oeuvres can be determined when you know how much time your guests will be standing around during picture taking, receiving lines, etc. Deli trays and/or sweet tables are nice if you elect to keep the hall for extra hours.

Understanding Bar Options

To open or not to open, that is the question. Many bridal couples today feel it is necessary to provide at least one hour of open bar service for their guests. But the legal as well as the financial aspects are constraining. My suggestions are:

Understand the liability laws of your particular county and state. No banquet facility is going to accept complete responsibility for the actions of your guests. Everyone involved can be at fault — the facility, the bartender, the waitstaff, your family, and you. But don't shy away from it all in a panic. We are talking about a wedding, and not an annual gathering of the Raucous Revivers of Good Ol' Ancient Rome. Most people will act responsibly. You can rest assured that your banquet facility has taken the time to train their employees to properly and maturely guard against such mishaps. (In some states it's an insurance requirement!) It is in everyone's best interest to be careful.

There are different options when hosting an open bar. Obtain from the function facility, in writing or printed form, all of the possible ways you can host an open bar. In some states where it is legal, you can have a per-person per-hour rate. Keep in mind however, that this option tends to work more in favor of the banquet facility. Some hosts pay for beer and wine, leaving guests to pay for their own mixed drinks. You can open the bar for the first hour only or, if you feel your finances can go one step further, you can allow drinks to be served up to a certain budgeted dollar figure. This gives you complete control over what you spend on drinks for your guests. Following the hosted service, a cash bar should commence, allowing your guests the opportunity to purchase additional drinks, should they wish to do so.

If you are considering an open bar, a good question to ask is: "If a guest simply asks for a gin and tonic, will a house brand be poured, or a more expensive name brand?" The latter is a rather unfortunate gimmick used by some banquet facilities to generate more income. Whatever the answer, you may wish to insist that name brands be used only when requested.

In any case, a good guideline for estimating the cost of an open bar for the first hour of your reception is as follows:

Multiply the anticipated number of guests by 2.5, then multiply that figure by the average cost of a mixed drink. For example:

$$200 \text{ guests} \times 2.5 = 500 \text{ drinks}$$
$$500 \text{ drinks @ } \$2.75 = \$1,375.00$$

Now add all applicable taxes and gratuities, and you have a very safe estimate of what your bar costs would be for the opening hour of your reception.

To estimate the cost of an open bar for the entire evening, multiply your total number of guests by 6 and follow the same format as above. For example:

$$200 \text{ guests} \times 6 = 1,200 \text{ drinks}$$
$$1,200 \text{ drinks @ } \$2.75 = \$3,300.00$$

As before, add in the proper taxes and tips, and you have your total. Of course, not every guest at your wedding will consume six drinks. But once you've figured the most it could cost you, anything less would be a blessing.

Remember that the **most drinks will be consumed during the first hour of your reception.** Be advised, a terrible amount of waste occurs. Guests will order drinks they normally would not. And in all the excitement of the cocktail hour, drinks are very often set down and forgotten, resulting in another quick trip to the bar. It's sad, but somewhat inevitable.

You may wonder if the bartenders are being honest. After all, they stand to make a pretty healthy tip for that one frantic hour of service. But let me assure you that hotel and restaurant managers are very particular about the people they employ. Any doubts still linger? Assign a favorite uncle or other worthy volunteer to stand by the bar during the hosted service. (Just remember that this person cannot be a key participant in your formal wedding pictures.) This guardian needn't act conspicuous — if anything needs to be reported, it should just be done as soon as possible.

General Beverage Information

Special Requests: Is your fiancé a Bud man? Does the best man prefer some gin blended only in Tasmania? Ask your sales rep if such items are available or can be ordered. Keep in mind that some facilities are licensed only with certain distributors, and it may be impossible to obtain your special requests. In many states it is illegal to bring your own beverages into a public facility. Be sure to find out!

Beer: Ask for a listing of all brands available to your guests. Beer is very popular, and the wider the assortment, the more people you will please.

Liquor and liqueurs: If the banquet room does not have a bar already built in (and most don't), your bartender will be working with a portable bar. And with limited space, the bar may be supplied only with popular request items. With this in mind, should any of your guests prefer liqueurs (especially as an after-dinner drink), ask if these are available and can be stocked for your wedding.

One last note before we move on. Beware of package plans offering open bar service for your guests included in the overall price. The function facility is obviously protecting their own interests when pricing out such an option, often resulting in your having to pay two to four extra dollars per person for drinks that were never consumed!

The Music

If a band is offered in a **package plan**, ask the following questions:

1. What is the name of the band and how many hours are included in the package plan price? (You should be quoted a minimum of four hours with an average of forty minutes on and twenty minutes off per hour. The band will coordinate their breaks with your reception activities.)

2. How long has this band performed at weddings at this particular facility?

3. Are all members consistent? (i.e., is the lead singer always the same?) Does the band rent itself out in parts — for example, is there a horn section that is not included in the package plan price?

4. How many in the group actually sing? (Having both a male and female vocalist is a nice plus. This gives you more range in selecting your dance music.)

5. Is there a videocassette or audiocassette available for your consideration?

6. Who is the emcee? What is the sales rep's opinion of the emcee's presentation and personality?

7. What will be the band's attire?

8. Will they play prerecorded music during breaks?

9. Will they learn any specific music they don't already know, if given adequate time? (If the answer is yes, you will probably have to provide them with the sheet music for any special song you want performed at your wedding.)

10. Is there any place you can see this band perform live? Often these bands will work lounges and nightclubs outside the wedding season. It may even be possible for you to hear the band performing at the function facility. But in such a case, remember to dress nicely and remain outside of the banquet room.

11. What is their policy and fee for overtime?

12. What happens if a band member becomes ill, or has an emergency on your wedding day?

13. What is the dollar amount subtracted from the package plan should you elect not to use the band?

If a DJ is offered through the package plan, many of the same questions apply as for a band:

1. What is the name of the DJ and how many hours are included in the package plan price?

2. How long has this DJ emceed weddings at this particular facility?

3. Is the DJ always the same, or is it an agency that sends out different emcees?

4. Is there a videocassette for you to consider?

5. What is the sales rep's opinion of his or her presentation and personality? (If the DJs are being sent through an agency, perhaps your sales rep could check and see if a particular "favorite" might be available on your wedding date.)

6. What would be the DJ's attire? Does he or she bring an assistant? If so, what does the assistant wear?

7. Does the DJ play prerecorded music during breaks? (This may seem like a terribly foolish question, but ask anyway. There are still a few disc jockeys out there who work exclusively with turntables and 45s!)

8. Is there a place in which to see the DJ perform live? (You may be able to attend a performance at a wedding at the function facility. But remember to dress nicely and remain outside of the banquet room.)

9. What are the policy and fees for overtime?

10. What happens if the DJ becomes ill or has an emergency on your wedding day?

11. What is the dollar amount subtracted from the package plan should you elect not to use the DJ?

Non-Package Plan Music

Quite a few facilities have deleted music from their package plans, based on cost alone. So, if you don't know of a band or DJ that is especially good for weddings, your sales rep should be able to give you some positive suggestions. On the other hand, if you already have a band or DJ contracted to do your wedding, ask your sales rep if the band or DJ can check out the facility for acoustics, loading access, etc. This is also a good time to ask if the facility has any policies regarding bands or DJs that you hire on your own.

For further assistance when you must locate your own band or DJ, please see the guide on page 65.

Feeding the Band and/or DJ

This is a special courtesy you should seriously consider if your budget allows. Of course, if you are paying an all-inclusive package plan price which includes the cost of the band or DJ, you should not be expected to pay the entire amount to feed them.

Ask your sales rep what the cost of each meal, without all the package plan "frills," would be with tax and gratuity added, or get a quote on sandwiches and soft drinks, or any other meal idea you or the sales rep may have for such a situation.

You needn't place the band members or DJ at a guest table unless you are personally acquainted with them and wish to include them in the festivities. Most performers prefer to take their breaks away from the crowd, anyway. It allows them a few minutes of peace and quiet without being bombarded with song requests.

Photography and Videography

If the facility offers a **package plan photographer,** they will most likely have a sample album for you to look through. As you browse through the pictures, don't just pay attention to the bride's gown or how funny the ushers look. Study the quality — particularly that of the special effects photos.

Then, make sure you know **exactly what is included and what the "extras" will cost you!** Now here's the unfortunate truth about many a package plan photography studio: They've offered the function facility a very attractive price to handle all their weddings, and for this "very attractive price," you may be offered only as few as two dozen color candids and an engagement portrait. However, that photographer is going to take roughly 300 pictures during the course of your wedding day. Are you going to settle for just 24 of these portraits? Of course not! And just wait until you hear the price of each additional picture you order! Ouch! Who made the best bargain here? Unfortunately, not you.

At this point, listen to what your banquet sales rep has to say about the package plan photographer. And be sure to get the answers to the following questions:

1. How long has this company been in business?

2. Roughly how many weddings has this particular individual or studio photographed for this function facility?

3. How many photographers and assistants are included in the package plan price?

4. What will their attire be?

5. How many cameras will they bring?

6. Will the photographer be at your home, the church or chapel, and the full length of your reception? (Note: If you elect to keep the hall for extra hours, you will need to contract the photographer for additional time if you really want him or her there. Many brides, however, find the costs prohibitive, and plan their final necessary pictures before the photographer leaves.)

7. Approximately how many pictures will be taken?

8. Does the function facility have a price sheet for additional pictures? If not, make sure you have the studio's phone number before you leave. You will definitely need this information before making your final decision!

9. Can you keep or purchase the proofs?

10. Who owns the negatives?

11. If the photographer is an individual not working for a studio, what happens if the photographer becomes ill or has an emergency on your wedding day?

12. What is the dollar amount subtracted from the package plan should you elect not to use the photographer?

Once you have gathered all the pertinent information regarding the package plan photographer, make a few phone calls to other studios in order to compare services and prices. Be a smart consumer. After all, it's your money!

Now, if a **videographer** is also included in the plan (presumably from the same studio as the photographer), many of the same questions still apply. But in addition, you will want to know:

1. What kind of camera and film will be used? Will the camera be equipped for low lighting? Will the film used provide a quality videotape when edited?

2. Can you work with the videographer in order to edit in some personal footage, such as pictures of you and your fiancé as children, your parents, and perhaps some taped footage from your engagement party and/or bridal shower? What would be the hourly rate for this service?

3. Can you keep the raw footage after it is edited?

Once again, it is a nice gesture to feed the photographer and/or videographer. They have been with you on your wedding day since an hour or so before your ceremony. Should you select to use the package plan photographer, obtain the price of your meal alone without all the package plan frills added in, or get quotes for sandwiches and soft drinks.

Should you need assistance in finding your own photographer or videographer, please see the guide on page 67.

The Limo

If a limousine is included in the package plan, be sure to ask the following:

1. What make, year, and color will the limo be?

2. Is it possible to arrange for a different model (such as a Packard) or a different color? Typically any upgrade would involve an additional fee, so ask!

3. How will the driver be dressed?

4. Does the individual or company offer discounts for additional vehicle rentals?

5. Is there a television in the limo? Just about every groom has asked me this question. It appears that many a wedding takes place during some "must see or die" sporting event, and these grooms think they'll catch a few minutes of it on the way to the reception. But don't worry. When that moment comes, he'll only have eyes for you!

6. Is champagne included? If not, and you'd like some, can this be arranged through the banquet facility or through the limousine company?

7. If the driver is not affiliated with a company that employs numerous drivers, what happens if the he or she becomes ill or has an emergency on your wedding day?

8. What is the dollar amount subtracted from the package plan if the limo is not taken?

If there is not a limousine included in your package plan, ask your sales rep for suggestions on reputable companies. **There are also some other interesting modes of transportation available. For ideas and details, see page 69.**

The Wedding Cake

If the cake is included in the package plan, your sales rep should have some pictures to show you. These sample pictures should display the various styles available with cake tops shown separately. You don't have to worry about how much cake you will need. The function facility will order it based on your final guest count.

Some questions to ask include:

1. Is the top tier real cake, or merely decorative?

2. Can you order something other than white or vanilla cake? In most cases there would be an additional fee.

3. How much in advance of the wedding day will this cake be baked?

4. Is a credit available on the cake top should you wish to provide your own? This is an area in which you can be creative! An array of ideas appear on page 73.

5. What happens if — God forbid — the bakery or the facility drops your cake during delivery or setup?

6. What is the dollar amount that will be subtracted if the cake is not selected from the package plan?

If the facility in question does not offer a wedding cake in its package plan, a guide to ordering your own appears on page 71.

Centerpieces

Most, if not all, function facilities offer guest table centerpieces in their package plans. They can range from a single rose in a bud vase to a spray of color-coordinated carnations to an elaborate bowl of floating orchids.

Often it is best to wait until you have investigated florists for your complete bridal needs before accepting the centerpieces provided in the plan. There are so many creative options these days, and the table arrangements at your wedding can be one of your very own signature pieces. **An entire chapter has been devoted to this and can be found in Chapter 6, beginning on page 77.**

In the meantime, ask your sales rep the following questions:

1. Do you have a choice of centerpieces included in the package plan price? (For example, if the plan includes a spray of carnations, could you have a single rose in a bud vase instead?)

2. What florist provides these centerpieces? (Get a contact name and phone number.)

3. Can you get a credit if you choose not to use the centerpieces, or put that allowance towards an upgrade?

4. Are candles allowed on the guest tables? This question will be answered by the fire and safety laws governing your particular county or state. In most areas, candles are permitted only when completely shielded by hurricane glass. And even then, you may have to hire a fire marshal to watch over the proceedings.

The Wedding Toast

Many plans offer a Chablis, rosé, or Burgundy toast with a small fee for an upgrade to champagne. With others, the toast is listed as being champagne. The truth is that in either case, the quality is not exactly what you might call "top shelf." According to your personal taste and budget, you may wish to serve a simple wine toast — especially when you can get a credit of 50¢–$1.50 per person for not serving champagne. You can always provide the head table and parents' tables with champagne, if you wish. No one else in the room is going to notice, or even care for that matter.

In any event, it is beneficial to ask if the waitstaff would visit your guest tables at the appropriate time and offer a ginger ale or juice toast instead. This is a thoughtful gesture for children and pregnant women. And there are always those who cannot or will not drink alcohol.

For the record, the shortest toast I ever heard consisted of one word: "Yo'!" The longest wedding toast was a nervously presented 25 minute history of the bride and groom's lives up until they met each other. Needless to say, the crowd was shuffling and yawning long before the mention of high school graduation. . . .

So what should a best man talk about? How the bride and groom met is always a good starter, concluding with what the groom said the day he told the best man he decided to marry the special woman of his dreams. Such sentiment is always a crowd pleaser, unless of course, it's done in a Sylvester Stallone impersonation lasting more than 20 minutes!

Linen

Your sales rep should have samples of all the available linen colors for you to look at. But buyer beware! Most colored linens, especially reds and greens, fade after just a few launderings.

This has always been an area of great concern for brides, and particularly for the banquet facilities who are renting these linens. At the hotel where I worked, we ordered three times what we needed in order to cull the best of each shade.

You will want fresh, crisp, matching, colorful linen. Speak frankly with your sales rep on this issue. You may find that going with starched white linen is your best bet. Never take on the task of providing your own linen unless you are personally acquainted with someone in the business. Tablecloth and napkin rentals can be very steep. And you, or someone you assign, must be responsible for making sure that every last piece of linen is accounted for and properly returned to the supplier.

Whatever the case, ask how the napkins are to be folded. Often the head table is decorated in a fleur-de-lis pattern, while the guest table napkins are fan-folded. This total effect is very nice. You will also want to know if the head table will be skirted, as well as the buffet table, should you elect to have one.

Reception Coordinator or Maitre d'

By this point in your interview, you may find your banquet sales representative to be a most delightful person. He or she is listening to everything you say, and seems to share all your hopes and concerns. You just might be wishing that he or she will be acting as your reception host or hostess on your wedding day.

The plain truth is, especially in large hotels and banquet facilities, these sales reps are required to work very long hours behind a desk. They come in well before nine, and are expected to stay late in order to accommodate appointments such as yours. In other words, the management has specific jobs for specific people, and acting as your personal assistant on some given Saturday or Sunday is not always a part of the plan.

Yes, I personally acted as hostess at the wedding receptions I booked. But that was my choice. Please try not to be upset if the sales rep you are becoming attached to cannot do the same. You will most likely find that the reception coordinator assisting you on your wedding day will be equally as wonderful.

In some establishments, the Maitre d' doubles as your bridal party host. This person has often had years of experience with the facility and, more importantly, with very special occasions such as yours. Maitre d's are chosen for their professional as well as their personal manner. And because they are in charge of the serving staff, you can rest assured that your guests will be treated as royally as you are.

Other facilities hire someone specifically to act as your reception coordinator. This person has no other duty than to attend to your needs and desires.

In any case, ask if there might be a convenient time in which you can meet your reception host or hostess. It is a common request, and you will feel better for it.

Safe-Deposit Boxes

Ask if there is a safe in which you can secure your money envelopes during the reception. Individually assigned lock boxes are the best. I do not recommend sharing a "common use" safe, which is one into which all the hotel guests have deposited their valuables. Unlike the other guests, you will not have complete knowledge of what you are depositing unless you open each and every envelope and count the funds.

Wedding Night Accommodations
(Hotels Only)

A complimentary room for the bride and groom is often provided in hotel-based package plans. No, it is not always the bridal suite or any one of the other top-notch accommodations, for that matter. But even if you do plan on staying elsewhere, this room will come in handy as a changing room, or even just a place where you can quietly freshen up during the course of your reception.

If you are dealing with a hotel facility, this would be a good time to ask about overnight accommodations for your guests. Many hotels offer affordable discounts for wedding guests, particularly on weekends — and you can include this information with your invitations. Just remember to find out if your wedding date coincides with a special event going on in or around town. This may mean that hotel reservations will not be available if you or your guests wait too long.

A guide to securing a block of rooms appears on page 81.

Cake Knives, Guest Books, and the Whole Nine Yards

Some packages offer some, if not all, of the specialty items you will need on your wedding day, such as:

* Place cards
* Matches
* Guest book and pen
* Cake knife
* Wine toast glasses

A few even offer invitations. In truth, many of these items come from the package plan photographer. And if you don't use that photographer, you may not get the goodies that go along with the plan. But don't panic. You will most likely wish to view a wider variety of styles when choosing your invitations, place cards, and matches. And as far as guest books, toast glasses, and cake knives go — you will probably receive these as gifts. Besides, the quality of the package plan equivalents is not always that great. If you don't get any or all of these necessities as gifts, you can easily locate what you need at any fine party supply or gift store.

Prices and Payment Procedures

Keeping in mind that your wedding is several months to a year or so away from the date of your appointment, be sure you know the following:

1. **Are the package plan prices guaranteed?** Most brochures will indicate the valid price dates, but always ask!

2. If you are not working with a package plan meal, **when can you be quoted final prices from the regular dinner menu?**

3. **Have all applicable taxes and gratuities been thoroughly explained?**

4. **Are there any other additional fees** for services such as room setup, bartender, or cake-cutting?

Have your sales rep provide you with an estimate of your total wedding reception costs. Remember, of course, that if you are interested in a personalized buffet menu, the sales rep will most likely not have an exact price quote for you as such menus must first be costed out by the head chef and/or the food and beverage manager. And an open bar, if you are considering one, can be only an approximation at best.

Just get as many prices quoted as you can that day. If there are any items needing to be priced out, ask that these figures be given to you as soon as possible in order to make your final decision.

And Speaking of Final Decisions . . .

Don't forget, the bottom line is:

* **How much and when is the first deposit due?**

* **What is the schedule for all other payments?**

* **What is the cancellation policy? When is any or all of your money no longer refundable?**

* **When is the balance due? Must this payment be made by certified check?**

* **How are any additional charges on the wedding day handled?** (Such as extension of the open bar, the last-minute addition of guests, etc.) **Is a credit card or personal check acceptable for such charges?**

And one last thing. If you feel in your heart of hearts that you might be interested in having your reception at this facility, ask how you may secure a "hold" on your requested room and time. Most places will offer to hold the space for you anywhere from three business days to two weeks without obligation (i.e., deposit). Of course, if you are given limited time to decide, and there are still items to be price quoted, you should insist on having a few days' extension in which to decide properly.

There! You have just concluded your first banquet facility consultation. Congratulations, bride-to-be! And now, to make things easier for you, I have compiled a summary of the questions you should be asking without all the "whys" and "wherefores" attached. You may want to make a copy of this and clip it to the inside of your notebook for easy reference.

Your Wedding Reception
Facility Questionnaire

* Name of facility:

* Contact person:

* Phone number:

* Date of first appointment:

* * *

* Name of banquet room(s) available for reception:

* General appearance of room:

   Rug color:

   Wall color:

   Are lighting fixtures working properly?

   Appearance of table linens (if applicable):

   Is the tone of the room too formal, or not formal enough?

   Where would the head table be placed?

   What is the maximum seating capacity for the head table?

   Would all guest tables be set in view of the head table?

Where would the band or DJ be placed?

How many guest tables are placed in close proximity to the music?

Where would the dance floor be placed?

Can the dimensions of the dance floor accommodate approximately _____ guests?

If the number of guests increases, would the dance floor have to be made smaller?

Where would the bar be placed?

* Where would pictures be taken?

Color of draperies in picture room:

Color of walls in picture room:

Dimensions of photography area:

* Does the facility have any plans to renovate any of these areas prior to the wedding date?

Guarantee of Room

* Can the establishment change the room assignment without your knowledge if your guest count changes drastically above or below your estimated number?

* Are any or all of the function areas handicap accessible?

Guarantee of Hours

* How many hours are allotted for wedding receptions?

* What is the fee, if any, for additional hours?

Food

* What are the popular package plan entrees?

* What are other possible entree choices?

* What are some of the choices for a buffet?

* If you choose a buffet, would a head waiter or waitress serve the bride and possibly others at the head table?

* Will a buffet table and standing area fit comfortably in the banquet room with approximately _____ guests in attendance?

* Is it possible to try the food?

* Will this food be prepared by the banquet chef?

* Would it be possible to arrange an evening to view the banquet room set for a wedding reception? When?

* If not wedding season, is there a formal dinner party setup you could view? When?

* What would be the cost, if any, of trying these meals?

* Obtain menus for hors d'oeuvres, deli tables, and sweet tables for future reference.

Bar Service

* Obtain information in writing regarding open bar service, if interested.

* What are the liability laws in regard to alcohol? (Check this also with the proper outside sources.)

* Are "call" brands poured only when requested by name?

* Are special request items available?

Bands (When Provided in Package Plan)

* What is the name of the band and how many hours are included in the package plan price?

* Approximately how many weddings has this band performed at?

* Are all members consistent?

* How many in the group actually sing? Is there a male and a female vocalist available?

* Is a video- or audiocassette of the group available?

* Who is the emcee or band leader?

* What is the rep's opinion of his or her presentation and personality?

* What will the band's attire be?

* Is prerecorded music played during band breaks?

* Will the band learn any special request music? Must sheet music be provided for them?

* Is there any place in which to see this band perform live?

* What is their policy and fee for overtime?

* What happens if a band member becomes ill or has an emergency on your wedding day?

* What is the credit off the package plan if the band is not used?

DJs Provided in the Plan

* What is the name of the DJ and how many hours are included in the package plan price?

* How long has this DJ emceed weddings at this particular banquet facility?

* Is the DJ always consistent, or is it an agency that sends out various artists?

* Is there a videocassette for you to consider?

* What is the sales rep's opinion of the DJ's presentation and personality?

* What would the DJ's attire be? Does he or she bring an assistant? If so, what does the assistant wear?

* Does the DJ play prerecorded music during breaks?

* Is there anywhere you can see this DJ perform live?

* What are the policies and fees for overtime?

* What happens if the DJ becomes ill or has an emergency on your wedding day?

* What is the credit off the package plan if you decide not to use the DJ?

* Does the facility have any policies regarding bands or DJs brought in by the bride?

* **If the music is not provided through your package plan, does the sales rep have any possible suggestions?**

Photography and Videography
(When Provided in Package Plan)

* Is there a sample album to view?

* How long has this company been in business?

* Roughly how many weddings have they photographed at this particular facility?

* What exactly is included in the wedding plan?

* How many photographers (and, if applicable, assistants) are included in the package plan price?

* What will their attire be?

* How many cameras will they bring?

* Will the photographer be at the bride's home, the church or chapel, and the whole reception?

* Approximately how many pictures will be taken?

* Does the facility have a price listing for extra prints, etc.?

* May proofs and/or negatives be purchased?

* What happens if the photographer becomes ill or has an emergency on your wedding day?

* Does the photography studio also offer videography?

* What is the price for videography?

* Are quality cameras and tape used?

* Can personal pictures and video footage be edited into videographer's material? What would the fee for this service be?

* Can you keep the raw footage after editing?

* What is the credit off the package plan if photography and/or videography is not taken?

* **If photography and/or videography is not offered in your package plan, can the sales rep recommend any reputable companies or individuals?**

"Service Help" Meals

* Get suggestions and prices for meals for your band and/or DJ, photographer and/or videographer.

Limousine (When Provided in Package Plan)

* What is the make, year, and color of the car?

* Is it possible to upgrade the make or the color of the limo? What would the additional cost be?

* What will the driver's attire be?

* Is there a discount available for additional car rentals?

* Is there a television in the limo?

* Is champagne included? If not, can it be arranged?

* What happens if the driver becomes ill or has an emergency on your wedding day?

* What is the credit off the package plan if the limo is not taken?

* **If limousine transportation is not included in your package plan, does the sales rep have any suggestions for you?**

Wedding Cake (When Provided in Package Plan)

* Are pictures available of the various styles?

* Is the top tier real, or merely decorative?

* May something other than white or vanilla cake be ordered? What are the costs?

* How much in advance of the wedding day will this cake actually be made?

* Is there a credit off the package plan if the cake top is not taken?

* What happens if the cake is dropped during delivery or setup?

* What is the credit off the package plan if the cake is not taken?

* **If the cake is not included in your package plan, can the sales rep refer you to any reputable bakeries?**

Floral Centerpieces (When Provided in Plan)

* Is there a choice of table centerpieces included in the package plan price?

* What florist supplies centerpieces? (Get contact name and phone number.)

* Can you get a credit on the centerpieces, or put that allowance towards an upgrade?

* Are candles allowed in the banquet room?

* **If floral centerpieces are not offered through your package plan, can the sales rep refer you to a quality florist?**

Wedding Toast

* How much more costly is champagne than wine?

* Is it possible to serve champagne at the head table and parents' tables and wine at the guest tables?

* Will waitstaff offer guests a nonalcoholic toast as well?

Linen

* What colors are available in tablecloths and napkins?

* Are linens fresh, crisp, and colorfast?

* Will the head table (and buffet table, if applicable) be skirted?

Reception Coordinator

* Who will act as host or hostess on your wedding day?

* If not the banquet sales rep, is it possible to meet this person?

* What will that person's duties be on that day?

Safe-Deposit Boxes

* Is there a secured safe in which gift envelopes may be placed during the reception?

* Is this safe shared with other guests, or are individual lock boxes provided?

Wedding Night Accommodations (Hotels only)

* Is there a complimentary changing and/or overnight room for the bride and groom?

* What is this room like? Is it possible to see it?

* Is there a discounted rate for sleeping rooms for your wedding guests?

* What is the procedure for reserving a block of rooms?

Miscellaneous Accessories

* Are any or all of the following provided through the package plan?

  ☐ Yes ☐ No   Invitations
  ☐ Yes ☐ No   Place cards
  ☐ Yes ☐ No   Matches
  ☐ Yes ☐ No   Guest book and pen
  ☐ Yes ☐ No   Cake knife
  ☐ Yes ☐ No   Wedding toast glasses

* Is a credit available if you provide your own accessories?

Prices

* Are all prices guaranteed for the date of your wedding?

* If not, when can exact quotes be given?

* Have all applicable taxes, gratuities, rentals, service fees, etc. been thoroughly explained?

Payment and Cancellation Policies

* How much and when is the first deposit due?

* What is the schedule for all other payments?

* What is the cancellation policy?

* When is any or all of your money no longer refundable?

* When is the balance due?

* Must this final payment be made by certified check?

* How are open bar charges handled?

* If there are any additional food and/or beverage charges on the wedding day, can they be covered by check or credit card?

* **At this time, have your sales rep quote your approximate total wedding reception costs based on your estimated guest count.**

Tentative Reservation of Wedding Date

* How many days can this date be held without obligation?

* Will a time extension be granted if certain requested prices have not as yet been quoted?

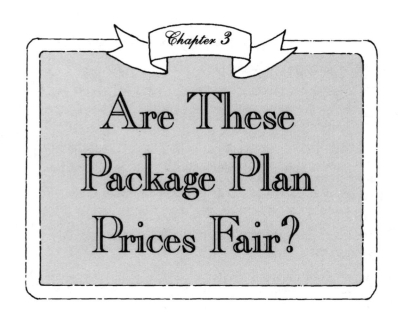

Chapter 3

Are These Package Plan Prices Fair?

An Interlude for Thought

With wedding package plans ranging in price anywhere from $25.00 to $125.00 per person, it is very easy to understand why a bride-to-be would question the value of what she is paying for.

It is relatively simple to make sure that the plan price you are being quoted is fair. It just takes some patience and a little homework on your part. The following easy steps tell you how, and the sample at the end of this chapter shows you how to add it all up.

1. Make a complete list of all the items on your package plan that you know the facility has to contract "outside" for (for example, band, photographer, limousine, cake, centerpieces, linen, guest book and pen, cake knife, and wine toast glasses).

2. Call at least two companies that offer the same services and get a price quote on exactly what the plan is offering you. For example, don't get a band quote on three pieces for two hours when the plan is providing you with five pieces for four hours. On the other hand, don't ask the bakery about a torte cake when the one the plan gives you is a three-tiered vanilla. Be

sure to ask if items are subject to tax and delivery fees. Delivery fees would most likely involve cake, flowers, and linen.

And when getting your linen quotes:

* For napkins: Add 50 to your total guest count. And don't forget to include the bridal party! You'll need napkins, too!

* For tablecloths: Divide your total guest count by ten. This is how many "round cloths" you should ask for.

* Add in 15 8-foot cloths to cover the head table, gift table, guest book table, etc.

3. For every item you are able to get two quotes on, take the average cost.

4. Accept your **meal** cost as it stands. You will have gotten this figure by asking your sales rep what it would cost to feed the musicians and the photographer. But if you do not have this figure, take your regular dinner menu and add $1.00 per person to the current entree price if your wedding is at least one year away.

5. For the **toast**, estimate $1.00 per person for wine, and $2.50 for champagne if you do not have readily available figures for this service.

6. Add applicable **taxes** and **gratuities** to all food and beverage services.

7. If the **reception coordinator** is someone who is hired from the outside, estimate $120.00 for this service.

8. If an **overnight room** is provided, call that hotel anonymously and ask for the rate of a room similar to the one you would be offered. Now, the Rooms Division rarely charges the Food and Beverage Department full price for the overnight room, so take the price you were quoted and divide it in half.

9. You might be charged a room rental for the **picture room** if you don't select the Package Plan. Figure in $50.00 for this.

10. Add in all **applicable fees**, such as bar setup, cake-cutting, etc. But keep in mind that if these charges are above and beyond the package plan price, they will have to be added as well, as the following graph shows:

Wedding Plan Cost Breakdown

A La Carte Wedding Plan

Service/Items		Cost
Band:		
5-piece/4 hours:		**$1,800.00**
Photography:		
Comparable plan:		**$850.00**
Limousine:		
Black stretch Cadillac:		**$295.00**
Cake:		
Three-tiered vanilla with top. Serves 200.	$395.00	
5% tax:	$19.75	
Delivery:	$20.00	
Total:		**$434.75**
Centerpieces:		
Head table and 19 guest tables:	$587.50	
5% tax:	$29.37	
Delivery:	$20.00	
Total:		**$636.87**
Linen:		
250 napkins. 19 round guest tables and 15 8-foot cloths:	$325.00	
5% tax:	$16.25	
Delivery:	$15.00	
Total:		**$356.25**

Guest Book & Pen, Cake Knife, and Wine Toast Glasses:

	$72.85	
5% tax:	$3.64	
Total:		**$76.49**

Boneless Breast of Chicken Meals:

200 meals @ $18.95	$3,790.00	
5% tax:	$189.50	
22% gratuity (food only):	$833.80	
Total:		**$4,813.30**

White Wine Toasts:

200 toasts @ $1.00	$200.00	
5% tax:	$10.00	
22% gratuity:	$44.00	
Total:		**$254.00**

Reception Coordinator: $120.00

Overnight Room: $62.50

Picture Room: $50.00

Bar Setup: $45.00

Cake-Cutting: $35.00

**Assuming 200 guests,
the per person total is:** $49.14

All-Inclusive Package Plan

$49.95 per person

Includes all services listed in the a la carte wedding,
with the exception of:

Bar set-up	$45.00
Cake-cutting:	$35.00

Total additional fees: **$80.00**

$80.00 ÷ 200 guests =**   **$ .40 per person
$49.95 + $.40 =   **$50.35 per person**

Compare this to the Package Plan which includes $.40 extra per person for fees. This represents an additional $1.21 per person, or a total of $10,070.00 when costed out for 200 guests, a difference of $242.00 more.

If you are dealing with a package plan that includes open bar for one hour, you should estimate your bar total as follows:

1. Take your estimated number of guests and multiply that figure by 2.5 which represents $2^1/2$ drinks per person.

2. Then multiply that figure by the cost of an average drink as this example shows:

$$200 \text{ guests x } 2.5 \text{ drinks } = 500$$
$$500 \text{ drinks @ } \$2.75 = \$1,375.00$$

Add in applicable tax (if not already included) and gratuity for your total. How does this compare? You just might find that the plan is padding a few extra hundred dollars into the cost to cover themselves for your open bar!

Now if hors d'oeuvres are also included in that cocktail hour, just take the applicable totals off your regular hors d'oeuvres menu, remembering to add in tax and gratuity.

Now That You've
Done Your Homework

If the totals rest within a few hundred dollars of each other, you will want to consider what this means to you, your budget, and your time. Is it worth the extra money to have the function facility take total responsibility for all of the package plan services provided? Or are you able to devote the time to making numerous phone calls and separate contracts and deposits, etc.? Are you willing to deal with any last-minute problems that may occur with the band, the cake, or the photographer? It's entirely up to you.

But if your carefully calculated homework shows a vast difference between what things cost and what the plan is charging you, definite action should be taken. Call your sales rep and have a heart-to-heart talk. If you can't get a satisfactory explanation of what all the extra money is for, you're probably better off considering another facility, or arranging for the service aspects yourself.

Whatever you do, be informed, be happy, be in charge. After all, this is *your* wedding!

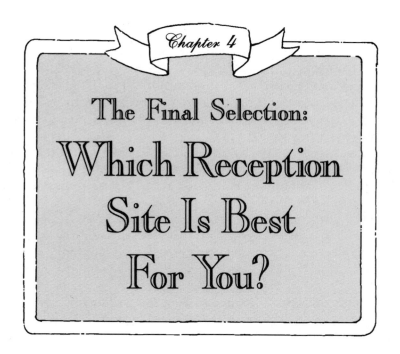

Chapter 4

The Final Selection:

Which Reception Site Is Best For You?

Narrowing Down the Field

Once you have visited all the banquet facilities on your list, you will need to call a meeting of "the powers that be." That is, the people paying for your wedding. Any additions to this group must be carefully considered, because, as the old adage goes, "too many cooks spoil the broth!" If the groom's parents are contributing, but not necessarily to the reception costs, you may still wish to include them out of courtesy — particularly if you have been close to them during your courtship with their son.

By this time, you should have a good sense of which facility or facilities you like best, based on your initial visits. And now is the time to "sell" this place, or places, to the others. Just remember (and this is the hard part, sometimes) that sticking to your budget is very important.

Now comes the next step, which includes:

* **Seeing the prospective room(s) set** for a wedding
* **Trying the food**
* **Hearing the band** (if included in package plan)

With luck, you will have narrowed it down to a few choice reception locations. Any more than this will result in some pretty hefty "dining out" bills. Then, call each banquet sales representative and ask when the next wedding is. If it's the wedding season, you should be lucky enough to view one that very Saturday. You will want to see the room half an hour before the arrival of guests. Please remember to dress nicely, as you will be placing yourself in areas where the reception party may see you, and it is wise to "fit in."

If you wish to try the food, ask if this can be done that same day or evening. You will most likely be asked to dine in the regular dining room. Arrange for a seating time that best accommodates the banquet chef.

The final step involves seeing the band you wish to consider. If you're in luck, it might be playing at that very same wedding reception.

An ideal outing would go something like the following.

Approximately 40 minutes before the wedding guests arrive, drive into the parking lot of the banquet facility. Does there seem to be adequate parking? (Remember, you should be there right before a hundred or so cars descend upon the place.) Is the area well lit? If it's too soon to tell, you can check this out when you leave.

Approach the hotel or facility. Are the grounds maintained nicely? Enter the lobby. Is there a function directory board in clear sight, listing the day's social events? Does it appear to be set up well? Are words spelled correctly? Does the lobby look neat and clean?

Approach the front desk. Are the clerks nicely attired? Did they look up and smile at you, giving some appropriate greeting? Ask where the room is you're about to see (they don't have to know that you could have found it without asking). Was the clerk's response pleasantly put, or in a monotone? Keep in mind that such things will be your guests' first impressions.

Viewing the Banquet Room

You will want to know from your banquet sales rep beforehand if there is anything in the room that may not pertain to your reception setup (for example, did the bride provide her own centerpieces and/or cake? Did the bride request the room to be set in any particular way contrary to the facility's suggestions?). Don't ever walk away hating something the facility had no part in providing!

Approach the Banquet Room. Has the hallway rug been vacuumed? Check out the place card table. This should be just outside the room, or directly inside. Is it skirted nicely, or clothed in a way that not too much of the steel legging shows? Is the linen crisp and clean? Are the cards arranged nicely? Is the guest book and pen in place?

Enter the Banquet Room. Is the lighting level attractive? (Note: if the banquet staff is still working on the room, the lights will most likely be set to full. You can see the appropriate lighting closer to the guests' arrival time. The same thing goes for the floor. Vacuuming is often the last thing done, so allow time for these effects.)

The Head Table. Is it set in a focal position? Is it arrayed with fresh, crisp linen and skirted or clothed attractively? How are the napkins folded? Is the silverware and glassware clean and shiny? Do the banquet chairs look comfortable and does the upholstery appear to be free of rips and tears? Does there seem to be adequate spacing between chairs (not too far apart, but enough to allow for long, full skirts and, in particular, your wedding gown)?

Guest Tables. Pretty much the same questions apply. Make sure that the linen appears to be fresh and clean with attractively folded napkins. Some facilities set the head table with more ornate silver, so check various guest tables for the condition and appearance of the silverware. Are the water glasses clean and spot free? Check out a few banquet chairs for rips and tears in the upholstery. You don't have to pull the chairs out, just push aside the edge of the tablecloth. Try not to touch the table setups. If the silverware is clean and shiny on the top surface, you know it has to be completely clean.

Centerpieces. (If provided in the plan.) Are the flowers fresh? Does the arrangement seem suitable for the size of the table? And, most important, do they appeal to you?

The Cake Table. Has the cake table been placed in an area of the room in which it may be seen but not accidentally disturbed? Is the table skirted nicely? Studying the cake matters only if it is a package plan cake, or from a bakery you may have been referred to. Are the tiers balanced nicely? Has the decorating been done artistically and carefully? Remember that although you may not like that bride's particular choice in cake top, design, and color, the artistry of the work is what counts.

The Gift Table. As with any service table, has it been skirted or clothed nicely, hiding as much of the table's steel legging as possible? Oh, and one minor note: If there are gifts already placed on the gift table, especially gifts that appear to be in the form of money envelopes, do not come in close proximity of the gift table unless a facility representative is with you. I am not suggesting that you would be dishonest. But if anything is missing later, you would not want to become involved in the controversy.

The Bar. Without stepping behind the bar, take note of the brands of bottled liquor and beers available. And is the bar itself clean and polished, or spotty and sticky?

The Dance Floor. Ask the banquet sales rep beforehand how many this particular wedding is set up for, or count the number of guest tables and multiply by ten (as an average number of guests per table) and then add in the number of chairs at the head table. Now take in account the size of the dance floor. Walk around the dance floor itself. If it is a temporary parquet floor, do the pieces seem firmly linked together? And the edging — is it on securely? Does the surface seem safe for dancing? It shouldn't be too slippery for stocking feet. Bridesmaids always seem to take off their shoes at some point in the evening! Is the floor clean and uncluttered by dried chewing gum?

The Staff. By this time, the guests' arrival should be very near. Does everything seem under control? Keep in mind that things often happen beyond the waitstaff's control, so a little "running around in a panic" can be pretty normal. It also means that they care about how things look when the guests arrive. You will know by their attitudes whether or not they take pride in their work. You may or may not be able to judge the staff's attire completely at this moment. Often, jackets and bow ties are donned at the last minute.

The Reception Coordinator. You should notice this person going about the room making sure that everything is being set up as planned. Do not interrupt unless you have arranged to meet at this time. You may, however, make note of his or her efficiency and manner. But as far as attire, once again, if the reception coordinator doubles as the head waiter or waitress, it may be the last minute before you see the complete wardrobe. Don't worry — the bride and groom will not be greeted by someone in rolled-up sleeves with a towel tucked into a belt!

If you have the opportunity to introduce yourself to the reception coordinator, try to understand if he or she does not have a lot of time to speak with you. Keep in mind that on your wedding day this person will be thoroughly aware of your needs and desires, so it is professionalism and personality you are judging now. Even if he or she seems a little rattled at the moment, take into account the situation. More often than not, last-minute instructions, such as changes in the guest table arrangements or event scheduling, have been called in, and the coordinator may have only minutes to deal with it. You will have more opportunity to see him or her at work when the bridal party arrives.

At Reception Arrival Time

As soon as the first guests arrive, you and whomever you've brought along should leave the room promptly. At this time, you will probably see the lighting set at a lower, more "romantic" level.

If you are dealing with a facility that offers a package plan **limo,** position yourselves outside, a safe distance from the front door, where you will be able to observe the driver's actions and courtesies in assisting the bride from the car. Be sure to note the driver's attire.

Then, after allowing the bridal party to pass, return to the lobby. Watch how the wedding party and guests are being greeted. You needn't feel awkward about being in the lobby, especially a hotel lobby. Any hotel guest who happens to be there is sure to pause and observe the beautiful bride.

The reception coordinator will most likely be gathering the bridal party for pictures. This is one area of the reception I do not suggest your trying to observe unless pictures are being taken in a public area, such as a pretty section of the lobby. But in most cases, bridal party pictures are taken in a private room. And the key word here is *private*.

Instead, return to the area of the banquet room and observe the cocktail hour from the hallway. Because of the constant arrivals, the doors to the reception room should be left open for a while.

There will be approximately 45 minutes to one hour until the bridal party is finished with pictures and is ready to be announced into the room by the band (who should be setting up by now). Once you have seen enough, or sense you are in the way, you may want to go to the lobby or the cocktail lounge and discuss among yourselves what you have already observed.

If it is at all possible to watch the bridal party processional, do so, but only if you can place yourselves where you will definitely not be seen. By observing the processional, you will be able to judge the reception coordinator's manner in dealing with the bridal party. You may also be able to hear the band or DJ's presentation. This is one of the most important duties they will perform at the reception. A good band leader or DJ will always come out into the hallway, introduce himself or herself, and go over the pronunciation of names before announcing them to the guests.

After the Bridal Party Has Been Announced

Typically, the doors to the banquet room will be closed so that the best man's toast and the clergy member's blessing may be heard without undo interference. Then the meal begins. This will most likely be the time you will be trying your meal, as well.

When trying the food, note the appearance of the plate. Is it garnished nicely, or somewhat thrown together? Is the food temperature acceptable? And is the seasoning too much? Too little? Are the vegetables freshly cooked to perfection, or all too obviously out of a can? (Remember that the time of year plays a big part in what vegetables are best.) And, most important of all, does the food appeal to you?

If you are considering the band that is playing at that particular wedding, return to the area of the function room after your meal. You may have to wait a while until the conclusion of dinner (you may even find the band on break at this time) but it will be worth it. After the meal, you can judge the popularity of the band by how eager everyone is to dance. Listen for as long as you can, noting:

* Is the band offering a variety of music for everyone's tastes?

* How is their rapport with the room? Do they just go about the business of playing music, or do they communicate with the guests and, in particular, the bridal party? The true test is if they address the newlyweds by their first names or simply as "the bride" and "the groom?" With luck, you will be able to hear them handle one of the events such as the garter and bouquet toss. How is their presentation? Are they encouraging the guests to join in? Even though you can not (and should not) actually see them, what you hear will tell you all you need to know.

When leaving the facility, check out the lighting in the parking lot. Do you feel at ease? Are the parking spaces farthest away from the facility's front door well lit? What adjoins the parking lot? (For example, is the banquet facility next to woods or another business property?) You will want your departing guests to feel safe and secure. If you feel at all in doubt, ask if the facility has surveillance cameras or a security guard in the evenings.

One bride I worked with arranged a lovely and elaborate dinner for her guests. But when her meal arrived it consisted of a hamburger, green beans, and whipped potatoes. . . .

When there are many people involved in planning your wedding, the meal selection (among other things) can become something of a headache. Is a compromise in order? Provide your guests with the type of meal your parents or in-laws-to-be are demanding, and then arrange with your wedding coordinator to have your meal (and the grooms) be exactly what you want. It can be done!

My experience has shown that many a groom will whine that he hates the vegetable you've selected for the wedding dinner. With all you have to think about, this little demonstration will probably make you want to strangle him. But don't. Call your wedding coordinator and ask if the groom's favorite vegetable can be prepared for his plate alone. Where I worked this was always done. It's a special surprise, especially for the groom who may have felt "left out" of many of the planning stage of your very special day!

Choosing the Winner

Once you have visited all the facilities that made the cut, you can at last make the final decision. Gather "The Powers That Be" and discuss each location in detail, noting what particular questions occurred to any of you during your visits. And, if at all possible, weed out the undesirable.

In the short time since your first initial interview with each function facility, certain questions may have come up that pertain to your particular wedding. Now is the time to prepare a list of these questions, as well. Of course, I can't predict what they may be, but here's a sampling of concerns to resolve before handing over that initial deposit to the banquet facility of your choice:

* Your flower girl and ring bearer are both small children and very, very fussy about food. What can be done?

Many times, a banquet facility will offer special meals for little children such as hot dogs, hamburgers, or chicken fingers. If this is the case, you will most likely be able to pick one of these offerings for any small child attending your wedding, so ask. As long as you meet the minimum number required for package plan prices, you should not have to pay package plan prices for kiddies eating hot dogs, but make sure, just in case.

* Your Great Aunt Rosie wants to make an antipasto to serve with the meal.

Regardless of which relative and what food, most, if not all, of the facilities that prepare their own food do not allow edibles to be brought in from outside. The reason is simple: All food and beverage establishments are governed by stringent health codes for your benefit. These facilities deal with food purveyors they have known and trusted for years. Now, we all know that Rosie would never intentionally bring botulism to your wedding reception. But the utmost control must be exercised, especially when the health of you and your guests is concerned.

* The park downtown has a beautiful magnolia tree. And if it is in bloom at the time of your wedding, you'd love to have some outdoor pictures taken there.

Any pause for pictures en route from the church to the reception hall must be coordinated with your photographer and limo driver. If these are provided to you via a package plan, ask your sales rep what the policy is regarding any side trips for picture taking. You will need to provide an idea of how far off the beaten track this picture location is for the proper response. Don't just say, "Oh, a few minutes," when it is actually 20 miles away.

* The best man's birthday happens to coincide with your wedding day. Could you hire a belly dancer to make a surprise visit?

Remember that although only the guests of your wedding will be in the function hall at that time, it is still a public facility, and certain entertainers — especially strippers — are not allowed to perform in public areas. Know your limitations.

* Instead of serving the wedding cake with dessert, you'd like to have it individually wrapped up and sent home with your guests. How is this done?

In most cases, you will be asked merely to supply cake boxes, napkins, or bags. Some facilities institute a nominal charge known as a cake-cutting fee for this service (if they're not charging you one already). Just make sure you know.

* You're having a completely traditional wedding and will be leaving by car at the conclusion of the reception. May the guests throw rice?

Even if the facility says "yes," your intuition should say no. Little birds cannot eat rice. It swells up in their bodies and kills them. Confetti is difficult to clean up. If such a tradition is important to you, and you are leaving before the reception is officially over, you may wish to provide little net wrappings of bird seed. In any case, the facility will most likely not allow your guests to throw anything inside, so birdseed is the kindest gesture.

However simple or silly your questions may seem, be sure to write them down. And with them, list the impressions and/or questions you accumulated during your second visit, when you saw the room set for a wedding and/or tasted the food.

Then call the facility or facilities (let's hope you're down to two at the most by this time!) and set up an appointment with your banquet sales rep. Do not, however, bring money with you unless you absolutely have to in order to secure the room. **Deposits should be made only when you have accepted all the terms of a written contract!**

For this appointment, bring along your fiancé and your parents, if you can. When you reach that final decision, you may wish to have their approval. Just remember to ask all your questions, understand all the answers, and know to the fullest extent all the costs, fees, and policies you are being faced with.

For those of you who might not have the band, DJ, or the photographer of your choice at this point, you may want to ask what happens if you cannot find suitable services. **Most facilities will allow you to transfer your deposit to another date without penalty, if done within a reasonable amount of time.** Just realize that if you don't have either of these services, you must get on it right away!

Have you found the place of your dreams? You will know it by the strange combination of calm relief and exhilarating confidence that you feel.

Congratulations, bride-to-be! Ask for a typed confirmation or contract of all the details, a signed copy of which you will send back with the requested deposit.

You're on your way to a perfect wedding!

Chapter 5

Alternative Reception Sites

Mansions, Yachts, and Gardens:
Hand Selecting Your Reception Services

kay, so you're the type of woman who shudders at the idea of a package plan . . .

It all began when you were seven and your silly cousin Myrtle wanted you to be her flower girl. Oh, that awful Little Bo-Peep dress! All you can remember about the reception is a sea of relatives' faces gnawing on assembly line chicken in a room without windows . . . and that band leader in the crushed velvet tuxedo! Well, that all may have been Myrtle's idea of bliss, but it's not yours! You want your wedding to be outdoors — unique — you want to be in charge! You and only you will hand pick the caterer, the music, the photographer, the limousine, the cake, and the florist.

If you believe the only way a thing can be done right is to do it yourself, then this is the chapter for you.

A hotel is by far the most convenient place to hold your wedding reception. Aside from the obvious food and beverage services they supply, hotels also offer overnight accommodations for the ease and comfort of your out-of-town guests. But if you reside in an area where historical homes, gardens, yachts, and museums rent out space for social functions, you may find such romantic surroundings more to your liking. Just keep in mind that you will have to be responsible for all aspects of your reception. But if you're patient, practical, and above all, organized, you should have no problem.

First, get yourself a notebook — preferably one with divider sections. Keep notes on everything and transfer important memos, such as deposits due and deadlines for decision-making, etc., to a calendar that you look at every day.

Make an appointment at each location that interests you. Each facility will have its own explicit set of rules pertaining to the use of the property. Most historic homes limit guest space to the first floor and grounds. And in many cases you will be required to provide a tent, regardless of what the weather reports promise for your wedding day.

Don't necessarily shy away from those places that insist on your using a caterer from their listings. At least you will be assured of contracting with a company that is familiar and comfortable with the working conditions of that particular property. And this saves you hours of phone calls and complicated guesswork.

Just make positively sure that you understand everything about the location you are considering for your wedding reception before going one step further. Will they allow the type of music you intend to have? Is smoking permitted anywhere on the grounds? Are food and drink restricted anywhere? If the facility limits your use to the first floor and grounds, make sure that your maximum number of guests will be comfortable indoors if it is raining on your wedding day. (The same applies to charter ships and yachts!) Is the facility air-conditioned? Is there good ventilation? And most important, do you have exclusive use of the property, or at least private use of a secluded area? Think carefully of all the questions that pertain to your wedding, and don't be afraid to ask them! Unlike the hotels in your area, these historical and specialty locations will be charging you a rental fee above and beyond all your other costs, so you must be perfectly content to follow their restrictions.

Caterers

Interview each caterer on your list. If the facility has no particular restrictions on whom you hire, you may still wish to get their suggestions on the best caterers they have worked with there.

Obtain all the menus you can, being sure to ask the following questions:

1. Is there a rental fee for equipment, above and beyond the cost of meals?

2. What is the condition and appearance of the equipment? Are the chafing trays plain or enhanced by a rococo design? (Plain

chafing trays will remind you of your high school cafeteria. The ones with a rococo design — that is, with scrolled embellishments on the legs and handle — are far more suitable for wedding banquets.)

3. Is real silver and glassware used?

4. What color table linen is provided? Are the napkins cloth or paper? Will the chairs be padded, or just regular folding chairs?

5. How many guests are seated comfortably per table?

6. What is the ratio of waitstaff to guests? What will the waitstaff's attire be?

7. Are all applicable taxes and gratuities included in the quoted prices? Are there any additional setup fees or charges?

8. When is the first deposit due, and how much is it? When and how must the balance be paid? (That is, can you pay by personal check or credit card, or must you get a certified bank check?)

9. What is the policy for overtime?

10. What is the cancellation policy? (Make sure you fully understand what happens to your deposit money!) Ask if you can view the caterer's setup before the next scheduled party at that facility. You will want to be there approximately 40 minutes before the arrival of guests.

Bar Service

If the caterer provides bar service, get a printed list of all the possible ways you can host an open bar for part or all of your reception. Remember that "portable" bars are limited in stock space, so if you know of any preferences you or your guests may have, inquire about their availability now. You will also need a wedding toast, so get prices for wine and champagne.

You can also provide your own bar service (if the facility allows). It's not as difficult as you may think, and definitely saves you money.

Ask the caterer if bartenders are available for hourly hire. If so, make sure that this includes all setups such as glasses, stirrers, bottle pourers, ice, fruit slices, etc. Most, if not all, caterers have bartender connections. But if the only way the caterer of your choice will provide you with a bartender is if they also provide the liquor service, don't give in just yet. If you know a bartender, either as a personal friend or by

frequenting a favorite restaurant or club, begin there. Sooner or later the right person will show! (Just remember that if you provide your own bartender, ask that person for a list of all the basic bar supplies that will be needed.)

To calculate your bar stock provisions, estimate six drinks per person for an evening reception. Not everyone will consume six drinks, of course, but you will want to be fully prepared. Deal only with a liquor store that accepts returns on unopened bottles. You will need one full liter for every 20 drinks poured. The manager of the liquor store will most assuredly assist you with all your needs if you ask. Having a good idea of the "age groups" attending your wedding will also help the manager in making suggestions about what you may need. And don't forget any special request items! You will also need mixers, juices, and sodas for those who do not drink alcohol.

When ordering your champagne toast, figure each bottle to provide eight to ten toasts. For wine, just order a larger quantity of what you will be offering at your bar, or provide each guest table with one nice bottle of wine designated for the toast.

It will be an immense help to assign someone to take charge of the liquor arrangements. This person should bring all beverages to the site and be responsible for explaining to the bartender that bottles should be opened only as needed. Then, at the end of the evening, this volunteer should gather up all bottles, separating the opened and unopened ones into different boxes. Unopened beverages should be returned to the liquor store for credit. And the partially full bottles can go wherever you designate. (Perhaps your parents' house?)

It may sound like a lot of work. But it will save you approximately half a standard bar bill! And with such savings, you might see your way clear to host an open bar for your whole reception.

What to Do When the Stage Is Set But You Don't Have All the Players

Finding the Right Band or DJ

Music is so important. It sets the tone and pace of your reception as no other aspect of your wedding day can do. The room can be dazzling, the food spectacular. But if the band is boring, you may find your guests sneaking off not long after coffee.

Decide first what type of music you would like to hear. The best bands out there can appeal to any age group and are willing to learn special songs when given adequate time. DJs have a wealth of music at their fingertips. Now, it's true that DJs were once disdained as not being "good enough" for weddings. But since those early days of record spinning, disc jockeys have become much more sophisticated emcees. You can now choose with confidence.

Begin by asking friends and family if they have any recommendations based on your preferences. Be sure to inquire at the facility where your wedding reception is to be held, for they will have seen many bands and DJs over the course of time. Often these performers have supplied the facility with a video for prospective clients to view. Just be courteous in returning the tape promptly.

When calling any prospects, find out if you are speaking to the band leader/manager, DJ, or a representative of an agency. Mention who has referred you and ask if they're available on your day, date, and time, making note of your reception location. If you are speaking with an agency, be sure to give the name of the DJ, band, or bands that have been recommended to you.

If all is clear, proceed with the following questions:

1. What is the fee, and how many hours are included?

2. What instruments are played (bands only)?

3. How many members in the group? (If DJ: Does he or she bring an assistant?) How many sing? Is there a male and a female vocalist?

4. Roughly how many wedding receptions has this band or DJ emceed?

5. What would their attire be?

6. How many breaks will be taken? Will these breaks be coordinated with your reception activities? Will prerecorded music be played during breaks?

7. Is there a videocassette or audiocassette available for your consideration?

8. Will they learn any specific music if you supply the sheet music in ample time (bands only)?

9. What happens if the DJ or any member of the band becomes ill or has a personal emergency on your wedding day?

10. What is their policy and fee for possible overtime?

11. What deposit is required, and when is the final payment due?

12. What is the cancellation policy?

13. Where can the band or the DJ be seen performing live? Will this be a wedding reception or nightclub date?

14. Would it be possible to put a tentative hold on their services until you hear them, either by live performance or video?

Call as many bands or DJs as interest you, and do your utmost to make your final decision as soon as possible. After all, you don't want to lose the best music you heard to another bride. And if you're getting married at a popular time of year, it could very easily happen!

Just beware of hiring musicians that have never emceed a wedding. Oh, they might play the best dance music you've ever heard, but who is going to announce the bridal party into the reception? Who is going to tell the best man when to give the toast, or command respectful silence when your clergy gives the blessing? You may know when to come out to the floor for your first dance, but who is going to gather all the single ladies for the bouquet toss, or encourage all the other fun aspects of your wedding reception?

Choose wisely. But choose soon!

Photography and Videography

For anniversaries and special occasions in the years to come, your wedding pictures will help you relive the memories of the most special day of your life. They are a legacy of your love, to be passed down to future generations. They are not to be trusted to just any studio or freelancer.

If you aren't fortunate enough to have a friend or relative in the profession of taking pictures, you will have to determine who is best for your budget and your needs. A "production house" studio, or a freelance artist? Both have their pluses and minuses.

A commercial photography studio will most likely be able to accommodate your wedding needs even when you have called a mere three weeks in advance. Why? Because large studio outfits employ dozens of photographers. Every one of these photographers has been trained to work the "company way." They know exactly what kind of picture sells and what does not. This is good, in a way. Good, if you want a standard wedding album filled with standard wedding photos. You see, your studio photographer will easily lead you through the paces of your "bride gets ready" shots. He or she will take those tearjerkers of you with Mom and Dad (for any good photographer knows who really buys these pictures!). Every customary pose will be included. The only problem is that when a spontaneous moment happens — such as the ring bearer painting the flower girl's face with mashed potato — your studio guy may be down in the lounge watching the Yankees clobber the Sox.

This is not to say that every studio photographer is a robotic bore. I would never insinuate that any human being is not entitled to a work break. I'm just saying that unfortunately, some production studio photographers may not seem as involved in your wedding day as you might wish.

And what of the freelance artist? He or she may have some fantastic ideas for those anything-but-typical settings for your wedding photos. You may bring the freelancer along on your trips to the boutique for gown fittings. He or she may inspire you to dress quite early on your wedding day and take pictures with the groom on a hilltop against the sunrise (that is, if you aren't superstitious about being seen in your gown before the wedding). Most freelancers will consider any "Kodak moment" for an hourly fee. And then you'll receive all the film for developing. Great! Great, that is, until your independent artist encounters an unforeseeable crisis on your wedding day. Then where do you turn?

Wherever your heart and budget may lead you, thoroughly investigate any photographer and/or studio before signing that contract! Beware of those "frilly" photography plans whose brochures are filled with more fluffy adjectives like "dazzling" and "breathtaking" than the hard, cold facts, such as how much those extra prints are going to cost you. See sample portraits. And, most important, **obtain in writing all costs and what they cover!**

You will also want to know:

1. How long has this company or individual been in business? Approximately how many weddings has this particular photographer covered?

2. How many photographers and assistants will be at your wedding? How many cameras will they bring? What will their attire be?

3. How many hours will be involved? Will the photographer be at your home, the church or chapel, and the entire reception? (Remember that if you wish to keep the hall for extra hours you will need to know all costs and policies for keeping the photographer late, should you wish to do so.)

4. Approximately how many pictures will be taken in total?

5. If you are considering package plan prices, what are the costs for additional photos?

6. May you keep or purchase the proofs?

7. What happens if the photographer becomes ill or has a personal emergency on your wedding day?

8. What are deposit and cancellation policies?

If the studio offers videography and you are interested, many of the same questions apply. In addition, make sure that quality cameras and tape are being used. If the idea interests you, ask if you might be able to edit in some of your own footage, such as still photos of you and the groom, video from the bridal shower, rehearsal dinner, etc. You will need to know the hourly fee for this service, and whether or not you get to keep the raw footage.

A special note: If you are leaning towards a photography studio but feel in your heart that all of the pictures you will want just won't be taken, do not despair! Simply call friends and family that you know wouldn't mind taking candid photos for you on your wedding day and supply them either with the proper film for their cameras, or those "instant camera" packs. Assign one person to collect all of the film at the end of the wedding, and voilá! A million memories that just one photographer alone could never be expected to catch.

The same principle goes for any one of your family or friends who owns a camcorder. Professional videography may seem too expensive with everything else you have to pay for. And members of the wedding can often get their fellow guests to "interview" a bit easier on film than a stranger can. Just make sure that the camcorder used during your ceremony can operate under low lighting (that is, if photography of any kind is allowed at your house of worship).

Limousines and Other Enchanting Ways to Get You to the Church on Time

During the course of one particular wedding season, I worked with three brides who fell victim to a horrid scam. They each responded to an ad in their local Sunday paper which offered a white Seville stretch limo for three hours for the incredible price of $100.00. Each bride mailed off her check by the cutoff date requested. Each bride received a confirmation call. And then, each unfortunate bride went to her wedding in the family Toyota. Needless to say, the phantom limousine company disappeared in a rich cloud of smoke.

Even Britain's Princess Diana had "royal" problems on her wedding day. According to Andrew Morton's book, "Diana, Her True Story," Diana's dressmaker had not taken into account the dimensions of the Glass Coach when designing that world-famous wedding dress. It seems the ivory silk gown with its 25-foot-long train was crushed getting into the coach despite Diana's careful efforts.

Call or visit only the reputable companies who appear in your local Yellow Pages. Get a printed list whenever possible of all cars offered, their seating capacities, and their rates. Some companies offer package plan prices for weddings, but get the hourly rates, as well, as they are sometimes less expensive. If you are thinking of hiring more than one vehicle on your wedding day, be sure to look into volume discounts. You will also want to know:

1. What is the driver's attire?

2. Is the driver's gratuity included in the fee? (Generally, it's 10%–15% of the total fee, if not included.)

3. Does the car have a TV? (Most grooms want to know this — especially grooms that get married during the World Series. Just humor him for now.)

4. Is champagne included? If not, and it appeals to you, what would the charge be?

5. What happens if the driver becomes ill or encounters a personal emergency on your wedding day?

Depending on where you live, there are other interesting forms of transportation also available to you. Some fully operating stables offer handsomely arrayed horse-drawn carriages. If you're considering an open coach, find out what's available to you if it rains. You can also check out the antique auto clubs in your area for some unique ways to get you to the church on time. (How about a string of midnight blue Model "A"s for you and the bridal party?) Just make sure that the car you travel in can accommodate you, your gown, and your handsome groom!

Whatever "royal" transportation you decide on, be sure you understand all deposit, cancellation, and final payment policies before signing on the dotted line.

Having Your Cake (and Eating It, Too!)

Once upon a time it seemed that all wedding cakes were three-tiered, totally white concoctions with little silver "things" all over it. Not anymore. Today's bride may want white frosting, but the cake filling and decoration often reflects her own taste and personality.

Browse through Victorian books and magazines for the most fabulous cakes you have ever seen. (The prices may also be the most expensive you ever paid!) Whatever the case and whatever the source, have a good idea what you would like your wedding cake to look like before heading off to the local bakeries. Bringing a picture is especially helpful.

Don't worry if there is something in it that doesn't quite suit you. If the majority of the design is to your liking, you can explain to the bakery what you would like to change.

Ask to see sample pictures of the bakery's work. Some bakeries even have "mock up" cakes on display. Do these sample cakes measure up to the picture you brought with you? Or, if you don't have a photo, do they measure up to the quality you pictured in your mind?

Ask what fillings can be done if you want something other than white cake or vanilla, and note the prices of those that intrigue you. Then be sure to get all of the following information pertaining to your particular choice or choices:

1. Are all three tiers real? (Some of those very ornate cakes actually have false tiers to cut down on expenses. Now, if you want to save a great deal of money, some bakeries will rent you a fabulous "fake" creation which actually houses a sheet cake under the bottom or largest layer, which you may serve to your guests.)

2. Are the pillars and tier dividers included in the price of the cake, or will they have to be returned to the bakery? (You will save a substantial amount of money if someone you know can return these items to the bakery for you.)

3. How much in advance of your wedding day will this cake be prepared?

4. Is there a delivery fee? If so, how much?

5. Does the bakery set up the cake at the reception site if the cake table is ready, or is the banquet staff expected to do this?

6. What happens if the cake is accidentally dropped during delivery or setup? (Note: If the bakery will claim responsibility only if they themselves do the setup, you must make sure that the reception site knows to have the cake table in place, fully clothed and skirted by the stated delivery time.)

7. Is it possible to sample the filling and frosting?

8. Is it possible to see the cake of your choice set up at a local banquet facility prior to the guests' arrival?

As with all services, know what the deposit, cancellation, and final payment procedures are. And if at all possible, use your credit card. If the bakery does not come through as promised, you may have some recourse through your credit card company.

On my very first day training as a reception hostess, I remember watching with fascination as three delivery men set up a rather elaborate three-layered wedding cake. How carefully they balanced those delicately frosted tiers! And as they stepped back to survey their handiwork — boom! — it happened. Apparently the table legs were not locked into place and the beautiful cake came crashing to the ground.

Within minutes, another cake appeared. And only after close inspection could I tell that this cake was completely fake. Of course I panicked about how the bride and groom would react once they tried to cut into this imposter. Luckily, it took only a phone call to the bakery and half an hour later for a duplicate of the first cake to arrive. The bakery would have to bake one more cake for Sunday's weddings, but now we were assured of a happy bride.

Cake Tops

Not enamored with the 1950s-style bride and groom dolls? Not crazy about doves, rings, and bells? There are always fresh or silk flowers (however, because they come in contact with food, make sure that your fresh flowers are free of insects and pesticides). Hand-blown glass tops are lovely and make lasting mementos. Or you can consider making your very own cake top — a personalized creation that means something very special to the two of you. A guide on page 77 tells you how!

A Rose by Any Other Name
Can Still Be Just as Expensive

or

All You Need to Know
About Wedding Flowers

Let's face it. Flowers can either make or break your budget. But it is *your* day, so you and you alone can decide to what extent you wish to be arrayed.

If you are fortunate enough, begin your florist visits one year prior to your wedding date. This way, you can investigate the floral possibilities in the season in which you will wed. In-season flowers are always less expensive than the hothouse varieties.

Always make an appointment with the manager or sales consultant of the shop. View their portfolios and ask for suggestions based on your budget, tastes, and needs. Ask if they have ever done a reception where yours is booked. If they have, the specialist may have some wonderful suggestions that will camouflage any undesirable aspects of the room.

Bouquets

Traditional bridal bouquets typically consist of orchids, gardenias, stephanotis, or roses. Always choose what appeals to you, but keep your height and figure in mind. The bridesmaids' bouquets generally follow the fashion of yours. If you carry a dozen long-stemmed roses your attendants could, for example, each have a single long-stemmed rose. One area of cutting costs on any bouquet is to make up for a lack of flowers with baby's breath and greens that complement the arrangement. Also, ribbons can be added that match your bridal party colors, but for a perfect match, you yourself should supply the ribbon.

Wire-wrapped bouquets are nicer and more natural. A plastic holder tends to feel awkward, and often makes your hands sweat. (If you do choose to use a plastic base, however, make sure that all the water has drained out of the arrangement before holding it close to your gown!)

Another important point is to make sure that you are not allergic to the floral arrangement of your choice. And don't just test the flowers! Hold the filler greens close to your face for a few moments and see if you have any reactions. True, you can always take an over-the-counter medication, but beware of the "spaced out," groggy feeling that some of these drugs may create.

You should also look into prices for a bouquet to toss. A smaller version of your bridal arrangement can be made as a keepsake for that special single lady who catches the bouquet. Or, if budget problems come in to play, ask the shop to show you samples of what can be done in a practical price range.

Boutonnieres

The groom may wear a single lapel rose, lilies of the valley, or a boutonniere spray of your bouquet arrangement. The ushers generally wear carnations that have been dyed to complement your bridal party colors. If the groom is wearing something other than a rose, the ushers may then wear roses.

Mothers' Corsages

The bride's and groom's mothers and grandmothers traditionally wear corsages. Orchids or roses are often the nicest selection. Just keep in mind each woman's height and figure. (In other words, don't encumber your tiny little grandmother with a spray of orchids that trail from her chin to her shoulder!) And the style of dress is also important. These ladies may not wish to be pushing pins through very expensive chiffon dresses. In such a case, you may wish to opt for a wrist corsage.

Ceremony Flowers

When considering what flowers should adorn your church altar, keep in mind the distance from which they will be seen. Sit in a pew a dozen or so rows back and evaluate what height is necessary to be seen with the bridal party arranged in the foreground.

One area in which you can save money is to ask your clergy if there is to be a wedding before and/or after yours. If so, you can contact these brides and ask if you might be able to share arrangements and costs. This is particularly helpful when your house of worship gently hints that the altar arrangements should be considered a donation to the church! If two or more brides are dividing the costs, the best compromise is to select white flowers when your bridal colors differ. Each bride should obtain a quote from her own florist for the arrangement agreed upon. The best price wins.

If you are considering having a flower girl in your bridal party, you may wish to avoid having her strew loose petals in your path. Not only might you slip and fall, but so might your guests. Depending on the girl's age, have a basket made of firmly secured flowers. A silk arrangement can double as a nice "thank you" gift for her participation.

Reception Flowers

The head table always boasts the most elaborate centerpiece. Just remember to keep your selection low to the table so that you can see and be seen. Additionally, ferns or other greens can be inexpensively ordered and arranged around the front and side edges of the head table. This adds color and acts as a base for your bouquets which should be placed on the head table so that your guests may enjoy seeing them.

Potted plants and flowers look nice on the "service" tables, such as the place card and guest book tables. They also make nice gifts for anyone you want to thank in particular.

Does your banquet room have hideous support columns? Encircle them with ivy. Large potted plants and other such arrangements can be used to mask those bland corners, or to "bring in" a room that seems too big for your particular crowd. As mentioned, your floral specialist may know the room your reception is to be held in. If not, arrange a visit to the facility and with his or her help, you can transform your reception hall into a paradise for very little money, especially if some of the "effects" can be rented.

If guest table arrangements are not included in your wedding package plan, discuss with your florist what options are available to you.

Many florists will rent bud vases to you in which you can place a single rose or a cluster of carnations that match the colors of your bridal party. But this can often create problems. Your guests may unknowingly walk off with the whole arrangement, which results in your having to purchase the missing bud vases at a price dictated by the florist.

As with every service aspect of your reception, select your florist with full knowledge of all deposit, cancellation, and final payment policies. You may look at various types of centerpieces, but if you want to put your signature on every table, check out the next chapter.

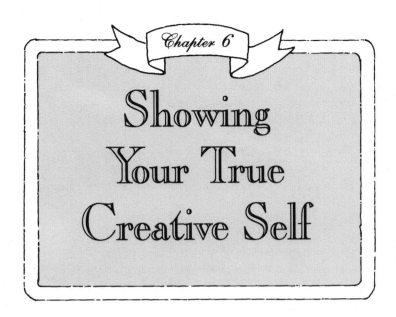

Chapter 6

Showing Your True Creative Self

A Guide to Designing Your Very Own Cake Top and Reception Table Centerpieces

Cake Tops

Sometimes it seems a shame to crown a beautifully handcrafted wedding cake with a second-rate cake top. The standard choices (generic bride and groom figures, feathery doves, and plastic bells) are rarely nice enough. But there are ways to complete a wedding cake that make it truly yours.

Are your parents still happily married and wonderfully in love? Then why not adorn your wedding cake with a very special bride and groom — your parents!

First, you will need to know the dimensions of the top tier of your wedding cake. Then find a picture of your parents on their wedding day and place it in a frame that complements the color and design of your cake. Hand-painted china or porcelain frames are lovely, and you can often find something with your wedding colors in it. Another solution is a filigree frame of silver or gold. This particular style would allow you to wire tiny tea roses or any other variety of small fresh or dried flowers through the openwork of the frame.

If one of your parents has passed on, you may still wish to consider this idea as a loving tribute. Discuss the idea with your remaining parent for approval. As long as it won't seem too maudlin (or create a problem with a new spouse) it's a beautiful way in which to have that very special loved one with you on your wedding day.

Another "framework" idea is to obtain pictures of everyone in the bridal party that will fit or be cut down to fit those $2^1/2''$ x $2^1/2''$ heart-shaped frames. Then you can ring the layers of your wedding cake with the faces of those you love best.

Now if these ideas seem too sentimental, or just don't fit your particular taste or style, there is yet another avenue you can pursue. Adorn your cake top with a symbol of your courtship. Not sure what to do? Well, it does require some thought. But something will come to you.

For example: is your fiancé a baseball fanatic? Was your first date at the home season opener? Is there a baseball player that your future husband idolizes to distraction? No problem!

Contact the sales office at your ballpark. (If they can't help you directly, they'll point you in the right direction.) Explain that you are getting married and that your future husband has been a fan of the team since he was in diapers. Now the real question is: If you offer to make a donation towards the team's favorite charity, will that special player autograph a baseball in bold marker with "Best Wishes to (bride and groom's names) on (date)"? Because you are making a donation, it is doubtful they would refuse. You can easily locate a stand for the baseball in any bric-a-brac store — perhaps an ornate filigree soap dish? And you can add that feminine touch by streaming ribbons to match your bridal colors from the base of your cake top down the sides of the cake.

Obviously such an idea won't work if your fiancé is a football or soccer fan. And maybe a baseball just isn't your idea of romantic. But you get the general idea. Sit down with friends and discuss the history of your relationship with your husband-to-be. Somewhere along the way, someone will have a brainstorm.

Yet another option would be a treasured figurine, such as a Hummel or porcelain Victorian lovers. But with anything so valuable, I would suggest assigning a friend or family member to bring the piece to the reception hall on your wedding day, and take it back the minute you have finished your cake-cutting ceremony. If all else fails, hand-blown glass or silk or fresh flowers can beautifully enhance your wedding cake. Remember that fresh flowers should be free of insects and pesticides.

Just keep in mind, however, that whatever the design, your custom cake top has to fit the dimensions of the top tier of your cake.

Guest Table Centerpieces

Flowers don't have to be your only choice in adorning the reception guest tables. Given your time, your budget, and your talents, a world of ideas is open to you. Are you hopelessly wishing you could have candles, but your state or county has restrictions on open flame? Well, you could ask your facility representative about the policy regarding "floating candles." This involves your supplying large brandy snifters in which a colored oil is placed. This oil supports a clear plastic wick which stays lit because of the oil. You can typically find inexpensive snifters at outlet bargain stores. The wicks and oil can be purchased wherever crafts are sold, and often the oil can be found in a color to match or at least complement your bridal colors. You'll have to assign some volunteers to set these up for you at the reception site. And for safety's sake, do not fill the snifters too high with oil. You'll want to avoid fancy dress sleeves from coming into contact with the flame. But, despite the effort needed, floating candles do create a lovely effect for an evening reception.

If your wedding date falls close to the holidays, you might consider table centerpieces with a theme. Pumpkins can be carved in interesting bowl designs to support wildflowers or other autumnal displays. Just make sure that your wildflowers are insect free. And the possibilities at Christmas time are endless. Poinsettias are typically inexpensive and make lovely centerpieces. Ringing the base of the pot with pine boughs makes a nice effect. If candles encased in hurricane lamps are allowed at your facility, create a wreath around each one with holly, ivy, or pine boughs with velvet ribbons to match your bridal colors. Brandy snifters can be filled with colorful glass ornaments, resulting in

a keepsake for each person at the table. You can also set up small Christmas trees, or baskets of arched pine branches that hold tiny dove and bell ornaments, symbolic of weddings. And to make your head table special, drape ivy across the front skirt of the table and attach big red velvet bows.

Whether it's Valentine's Day or not, think hearts. Fill brandy snifters with colorful candy hearts. Then encircle the snifters with ivy and attach heart-shaped ornaments to the twine so that each heart lies flat on the table facing a guest's chair. Once again, a loving keepsake your guests will always treasure.

This next idea is time consuming. But the rewards are worth the effort.

Take your guest list and group people as you would place them at guest tables. You will have friends from work, friends from college, relatives, neighbors, etc.

Now consider each "table group" separately and decide what it is that draws you all together. For example, your business friends — do you all work together, say in a secretarial pool? Then find a toy typewriter and attach balloons to the keys that match your bridal party colors. Did you and your college friends have a favorite hangout? Even if it's out of state, call that restaurant, pub, or whatever — explain that you're getting married etc. — and ask if they'll mail you a menu or something with the establishment's name on it. Then ask your reception facility if you can borrow a table display holder (the coiled chrome or clear plastic device that restaurants use to display wine lists and dessert specials). If they don't have one, they should be able to refer you to a restaurant supply store that does. Then, on your wedding day, your college buddies will have a grand time recalling the good ol' days. Make a painted cardboard copy of your street sign for the neighbor's table and attach balloons through small punch holes in the sign.

Family pictures are nice for the parents' tables. As mentioned in the "Cake Top" section of this chapter, filigree frames can be enhanced with fresh or dried flowers. And porcelain frames can be found to match your bridal colors.

Are you worried that a room full of balloons, bells, and baseballs will seem rather chaotic? Don't be afraid of your wedding day being less than uniform. It's a festive day and the joy you will create by making your guests feel cherished and special will be remembered for years to come!

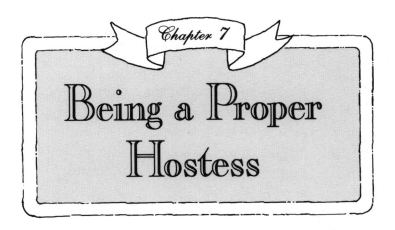

Chapter 7

Being a Proper Hostess

Finding Hotel Accommodations for Out-of-Town Guests

always seem to be pushing hotel facilities as the best all-around location for a wedding reception. This is simply because they offer the most for your money. And overnight rooms for your guests is another one of those pluses.

But whether or not the facility of your choice is a hotel, you will need to provide your out-of-town guests with some idea of where they can stay. Even your local guests may wish to avoid the risk of driving home after having a few drinks at your reception.

Call for rates early! In the first place, you tend to get a better rate when calling a year or so in advance. And once a rate is quoted, it's golden. Second, if your wedding date happens to fall on a convention weekend, or during fall foliage or any other special event, you will need to know this as soon as possible so that your guests who will need rooms can get them!

If your reception is booked at a hotel, contact your banquet sales representative. In larger operations, you might be referred to a Group Sales Manager. In any case, you will want to get information on rates for the day before, the day of, and the day after your wedding. And, if you are speaking with a representative of the hotel other than the banquet sales rep, you will want to point out that your wedding is being held there. Be sure you know the following:

1. (Based on your wedding occurring on a weekend) Is this the best weekend rate available? Is there an additional discount if a certain number of rooms are booked by your wedding guests?

2. (Based on your wedding occurring during a weekend) What would the weekday rate be per night for guests arriving earlier in the week, or staying later into the next week?

3. Are these rates per person or per room?

4. What is the rate with tax? Are there any other fees or surcharges?

5. What is the cost for cribs? For rollaway beds?

6. Are handicapped rooms available?

7. Are there any special events coinciding with the weekend (or surrounding the date) of your wedding?

8. Is there a toll-free reservation number that out-of-state guests can call direct to reach the hotel?

9. Up until what time of day can a room be held for guest arrival without a credit card number to secure it?

10. What credit cards are accepted at this hotel?

If the hotel sees no danger of filling up well before your wedding guests have received their invitations:

* Ask that a "rate quote" card be filled out with your name (use your maiden name), the groom's name, and the weekend or date of your wedding. This method does not guarantee rooms for your wedding day, so you have no financial obligations. It simply provides the reservationist with the proper rate quote for your group. You will be responsible for supplying any necessary information to your guests. But don't worry — it's very simple!

* Ask if you may have some brochures to mail to your guests. These should be supplied to you without charge. Ask for enough for one-half of your total guest count.

The best plan of action is to mail the hotel brochure separately from your invitation, with the rate information for all guests, and a list of "tourist activities" included for those coming from out of town.

Your hotel information notice can be simply typewritten, copied, and folded into the brochure. Here's an example:

THE BELMONT PLAZA
of Belmont Hills, Massachusetts

is pleased to offer specially discounted rates
for our wedding guests!

$49.00 per room per night on the weekend
(**$55.00** per room per night during the week)
plus 9.7% tax

In-state call direct: Out-of-state call toll free:
(617) 555-1776   **1-800-555-0001**

Remember to tell the reservationist that you are with the
Hamilton-Cartwright Reception

A VISA®, MasterCard®, American Express®, or
Diners Club Card® number will be necessary
to hold your room for arrival after 4 p.m.

Call early to ensure availability!

See? It's that easy!

But what if there is a special event scheduled for the same weekend as your wedding? If rooms are currently available, you should definitely reserve a "block" of rooms for the ease and comfort of your guests.

How many rooms will you need? The average wedding results in 10% of the guests booking rooms. So, if your anticipated guest count is 200, reserve 20 rooms. However, if you plan on inviting several out-of-town guests, increase that number accordingly!

Avoid using your credit card to hold a block of rooms. Instead, get a cut-off date. This simply means that these 20 or so rooms will be held until a certain date without obligation. On that specified date, any and all unclaimed rooms in your block are released for public sale. Any request for reservations made by your wedding guests after the cut-off date would then be subject to availability.

Keep in mind that you will have to give your guests adequate notice! If your cut-off date is five weeks prior to your wedding, you must send your invitations out approximately eight weeks before your wedding day!

You can send out a notice like the example shown in this chapter, but remember to replace the "Call early to ensure availability" line with something like the following:

PLEASE NOTE:
Due to the increased demand for rooms during fall foliage season, you must make your reservations prior to September 1st!

In any case, remember that you will want to book rooms for your bridesmaids, ushers, and other important friends and family members coming from out of town. Count up the number of rooms you know you will need and add half a dozen to that number. Remember to ask for nonsmoking rooms for your friends and family who do not smoke.

Give a credit card number to hold these rooms and get a written copy or computer print-out of your reservation. This should state the latest date you can cancel what you don't need. Securing the six extra rooms helps in two ways: (1) You may have unintentionally forgotten someone special on your list. (2) Because of your credit card hold, these rooms will be available longer than the general block of rooms held for your wedding guests. In this way, you might be able to assist anyone who waited until the last minute to get a room. **Just remember to cancel what you don't need by the date specified!** If you don't, your credit card will be billed for at least one night's room and tax on any and all unclaimed rooms. And if the hotel can prove that you understood the policies, you will have little or no recourse through your credit card company.

Now, if your reception facility does not have overnight accommodations, call or visit all the hotels, motels, inns, and bed-and-breakfast facilities in your immediate area. Get rate quotes for your wedding day and ask if the facility has a toll-free number. I would recommend taking the time to see a guest room at each facility. This helps you to avoid referring a property to your guests that might not be quite up to your standards.

Type a list of all the accommodations, indicating the phone numbers and rates quoted. Depending on the style and mailing specifications of your invitation, you can either include this list as an insert to your invitation, or mail it separately with a "tourist activities" list for out-of-town guests. And, as previously mentioned, if your wedding date coincides with a special event in your area, indicate to your guests that they should make their reservations as early as possible.

Having reviewed all of the overnight accommodations in your area, select the best site for your bridesmaids, family members, or whomever you will be providing rooms for, based on where you believe they might feel most comfortable. Bed-and-breakfasts often appeal to couples, and many of these homes or small inns provide truly romantic atmospheres. They are not, however, always suitable for a group of giggling bridesmaids. Your friends might wish to "party" and have a good time, and may not feel quite at ease doing so in someone else's home. Just use your best judgment. Not all your personal guests need to stay at the same place.

And once again, as tiresome as it may be to hear, remember to get in writing all the deposit and cancellation policies!

Tourist Activities for Out-of-Town Guests

Once your closest friends and family from out of town hear the happy news of your engagement, they may possibly decide to work their vacation plans around the day of your wedding. And even for those just coming for the weekend, what nicer gift can you give them but some great ideas on what to do!

If you, your fiancé, or any immediate family member belongs to AAA, or any other fine travel service, you're in great luck. Visit your local office, explain that you're getting married, etc., and ask for information on all there is to do within easy driving distance in the season in which you will wed. Know in advance approximately how many mailings you would need. Some agencies will have stock supplies of brochures, coupons, etc., just for the asking.

I once worked with a bride who didn't have to give a moment's thought as to what her guests could do for fun and recreation. You see, the Boston Red Sox were in the pennant race, and nearly all of New England had gone mad. Guests brought portable televisions and hid them under the guest tables. But the bride's father was even bolder. He had a small battery-operated TV set right at his place at the head table! At first, I was mortified. The bride was in tears and I didn't know what to do. The band kept announcing the score to great cheers in the room, and after dinner all those "tucked away" televisions made their way to the guest tables. But do you want to hear something very strange? There was camaraderie that day — a sense of spirit — that I have never seen before or since. The bride began to have a great time with it all, and so did I. The Red Sox made a fabulous ninth-inning win, and I had the pleasure of hosting the best wedding reception of the year!

Even if you don't have any professional contacts in the travel world, there are still some options open to you:

* Visit your local Chamber of Commerce for ideas.
* Drive to your closest tourist information facility.

If you have no way of getting, or for that matter mailing, all of the tourist information available to your guests, you can simply type a list and send it out with your hotel notice. Just remember to include a variety of activities and restaurants to appeal to both couples and families. And for courtesy's sake, include church service schedules for as many denominations as you can. (Note: If your reception is being held at a hotel, the front desk usually has, or posts, such a listing. You can either copy this information, or indicate on your packet that the hotel will provide schedules upon request.)

If you have enough time and the desire to do so, you can write your own **Personal "Travel Guide"** for out-of-town guests! Just visit all the fun places to go to in your area (if you haven't done so recently) and write your opinions down in letter format to copy for your guests. Be sure to include everything — amusement parks, museums, walking tours, aquariums, historic buildings, beaches, gardens, nature trails. . . . Are there any interesting arts and crafts galleries, or any other specialty shops, particularly in "restored" areas? What sporting events are going on? Are there any special celebrations in or around town, such as a bluegrass festival or Oktoberfest? Is there a lovely dairy farm nearby that offers tours of their cheesemaking process? How about bicycle tours, or boat rides? Just keep in mind the time of year in which your wedding will occur. And for basic information, list movie theatres and local restaurants. If you have a favorite romantic or fun restaurant, be sure to let people know, but also include the "family" type eateries so that everyone can dine well according to their budgets.

This personalized travel planner can be as informative and as fun as you want to make it. And don't be afraid to ask each place for coupons you can pass along to your guests (restaurants included). They'd most likely welcome the added business. And your wedding guests will feel honored that you did so much to make their stay special!

One suggestion for making your out-of-town guests feel just how happy you are to have them at your wedding is to provide them with all the essentials for a picnic. Line a pretty paper bag or a basket with colored tissue paper. Then fill the bag with all sorts of goodies — bubbly water or juice, cheese and crackers, fruits, nuts, and chocolates. If the weather is appropriate they can venture outside and take in some of the local sites and enjoy a picnic. But, if the weather is too cold or rainy for an outside picnic, they can always make themselves comfortable in their room and enjoy your treats.

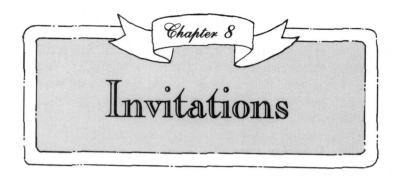

Chapter 8

Invitations

The Pleasure of Your Company

emember that guest list you were working on with "the powers that be"? Well, now it's time to tackle the arduous task of getting out your wedding invitations.

Since the announcement of your engagement, you've probably been hard at work perfecting your guest list. More likely, you've been pulling your hair out over the way your guest list is going, especially if your parents have had anything to do with it.

You see, parents have a penchant for wanting to invite all their friends and business associates to your wedding. And when you ask them why, parents always say, "Because they invited us to their daughter's wedding." Now, this isn't always the whole truth. Your parents are proud of you. They want to gloat. They want to brag, "See? We got her this far!" And, if your parents are contributing solely, or even in an equal manner, to your wedding, they have a right to all, a half, or a third of the guest list. Way back in the very first chapter of this book, I talked about learning how to compromise. Well, grit your teeth and try to smile. This is it.

When more than one person controls the guest list, things get frustrating. It's a plain fact, and you must deal with any problems accordingly. My suggestion is that any person who wishes to invite more than his or her allotted amount should personally pay for those additional guests. Just remember to keep within the capacity limits of your banquet room!

Now what if you have eight wonderful friends at work that you definitely want to invite, but including their spouses puts a strain on your wallet. By all means, invite those friends. Just let them know verbally as soon as possible that you're sorry, but your budget doesn't have room for extra people at this time. You might make an exception if you are very good friends with one or more spouse or "significant other." Certainly include them if you can. The others should understand.

Should you invite your boss? For the same reason your mother and father want to include theirs, you might want to consider doing the same. Inviting the boss is good for business. Now, I don't suggest sending an invitation to some high-powered executive whom you've never seen. But if your direct supervisor is a decent person — did he or she bend over backwards to get you extra time off for your honeymoon? — then definitely invite them. And this is one of those exceptions where you should include a spouse or companion.

The only other time I would suggest sending an invitation that includes "and guest" is when the person you are inviting is not acquainted with anyone else at your wedding and may feel terribly awkward attending alone.

And what about children? If you are inviting a lot of couples with children, it is best not to include any kids at all (with the exception of your flower girl and ring bearer, of course). Simply address your invitation to "Mr. and Mrs. Robert Jones." Sending an invitation to "Mr. Robert Jones and Family" indicates that you wish to include everyone in the festivities.

If an entire family is planning their vacation around your wedding — and that means the children are coming — the decision is entirely up to you. If you don't care that a few disgruntled parents will be muttering under their breath, fine. But there's an even happier solution to this problem: If your reception is being held at a hotel, provide a babysitter. The safest option is to contact someone you know from your neighborhood. Most hotel facilities offer babysitting service with advance notice, as well. And although this employee may be honest and trustworthy, I would always opt to place children with someone you are comfortable with. Everyone will feel better for it and have a worry-free time at your wedding.

Selecting Your Invitations

The days of black print on white stock are long gone. Today's bride has a wider selection than ever of styles, colors, and ink shades. And anything from Victorian scented scrolls to electric purple laminate goes! The choice is yours, lucky bride. Happy hunting.

Seriously, however, you should visit as many print shops as you can and view their sample books with your style of wedding in mind. Will it be formal or festive? Black tie or barbecue? This should assist you

For the older bride, or second time marriage, the presence of children at your reception may be an inevitable factor to deal with. One suggestion is to rent a separate room at your reception facility. Hire someone to entertain the kids — a clown, DJ, or children's theatre troupe — whatever your budget and the age group permits.

Feed the children hamburgers or pizza, and then invite them to join you after the formal meal has been served. By this time their level of activity will fit in a bit more easily with the rest of the wedding.

If you can't afford such an elaborate setup on your own, ask the maid of honor to send a flyer to all the guests who have children informing them about the alternative food and entertainment for children and the cost per child. Don't be embarrassed to ask for help! After all, these parents would most likely have to arrange for babysitting one way or another. This kind of a deal might just work out to be less money and a lot more fun for all involved!

in deciding what stock and printing style convey your message best. Study each variety of wording for the one that says it all for you. You needn't feel concerned if each and every sample says "Mr. and Mrs. Allen Smith requests the honor of your presence at the wedding of their daughter. . . ." The wording of the host line is determined by your own personal situation and needs.

When getting your price quote, add 50 to the total number you think you will need. This provides you with leeway for mistakes and/or extras for any last-minute additions. The golden rule of printing seems to be that the more you print the less per invitation it will cost. You may find that ordering a hundred extra invitations doesn't add any significant amount to the price.

Colored inks add to the cost of your invitations. If the sample that catches your eye is printed in dusty rose, compare what the same one would be with standard black ink.

One cost-cutting option is to contact local technical schools about printing your invitations. Just make sure that they can do all the inserts you need, and in the time frame you need them. And allot time for proofreading.

Proofreading is a funny thing. We're all very particular about checking the spelling of our names, but we aren't as meticulous about the wedding date and ceremony time. We assume the printer can spell the state we live in, so we don't look very carefully. **That's a mistake.** Be certain to carefully proofread the information you give to the printer. When you receive the invitations, proofread them again to be sure they are correct.

Never proofread when tired. Share the duty. Block each and every word with the blank side of an index card if you have to in order to concentrate. Even read it backwards — once you say "print," you pay.

In any event, get your invitations printed early. It is far more relaxing to address them at your leisure than to wait until the last minute when every other detail of your wedding seems so pressing.

Who is the Host?

Traditionally, the bride's parents are the host and hostess of the wedding, and the opening line of a wedding invitation reads something like this:

Mr. and Mrs. Martin Leigh

request the honor of your presence

at the marriage of their daughter

Jessica Ann

(and so on)

Now, if your mother has remarried:

Mr. and Mrs. Jonathan Spencer
request the honor of your presence
at the marriage of Mrs. Spencer's daughter
Miss Jessica Ann Leigh

If your father has remarried, and is the primary host:

Mr. Martin Leigh
requests the honor of your presence
at the marriage of his daughter
Jessica Ann Leigh

If your parents are divorced and have new spouses, but are on friendly enough terms to host your special day together:

Mr. Martin Leigh and Mrs. Jonathan Spencer
request the honor of your presence
at the marriage of their daughter
Jessica Ann

(include your last name if desired)

Here's the tricky one. If your divorced parents are hosting your reception together, but only your father has remarried, you will want their approval on how the invitation is worded. To call them Mr. and Mrs. Martin Leigh may cause your guests to assume that the second Mrs. Leigh is acting as hostess. Your mother could, if so desired, utilize her maiden name to distinguish herself from your father's new wife, either allowing her maiden name to stand by itself, or by hyphenating it with "Leigh." You can even drop the "Mr." and "Mrs." part, such as shown here:

Martin Leigh and Victoria Allen-Leigh

Whatever the case, let your mother be comfortable with the wording. If your parents are deceased, and a family member (such as an uncle) is assisting you with your plans, the wording could read something like:

Mr. Andrew Leigh

requests the honor of your presence

at the marriage of his niece

Jessica Ann Leigh

If you and the groom are solely doing the inviting, your names simply head the invitation. You can dispense with the "Miss" and "Mr." if you prefer:

Jessica Ann Leigh and Robert Dean Williams

request the honor of your presence

on the occasion of their marriage

When the groom's parents act as host:

Mr. and Mrs. Roy Williams

request the honor of your presence

at the marriage of their son

Robert Dean Williams

to

Jessica Ann Leigh

And, finally, if all parents are alive, happily married, and want to share the spotlight:

Mr. and Mrs. Martin Leigh

and

Mr. and Mrs. Roy Williams

request the honor of your presence

at the wedding of their children

Jessica Ann and Robert Dean

(add your last names, if desired)

All of these are merely suggestions. You will know what suits your needs the best. Don't fuss over etiquette and tradition just because you think you have to. The best invitation need only speak from your heart!

When to Mail Your Invitations

* **For Thanksgiving and Christmas time weddings:** Phone important family members and friends as soon as you have selected the date. Then mail all your invitations four months ahead of schedule.

* **For weddings occurring over long weekends:** Once again let close friends and family know as soon as you do. Then mail all invitations three months in advance.

* **If your wedding coincides with a "special event" in town:** Give your guests ample opportunity to find hotel rooms if they need them. (See the previous chapter on hotel accommodations.) Send your invitations approximately two to three weeks in advance of the last available day to make sleeping room reservations.

* **If your nuptials occur during a popular month for weddings, such as September or October:** Send out all invitations eight to ten weeks in advance.

* **For all others:** Six to eight weeks is acceptable.

The latest trend in "celebrity marriages" is to invite guests to a cookout or christening that turns into a wedding. The purpose is to keep the press from catching wind of the nuptials, but the "foil" isn't practiced by the rich and famous alone. Many couples embarking on a second marriage, or those who just don't want the fuss, choose the same kind of marvelous deception. A creative caterer can assist you with your established theme. Or, for those bridal couples who don't wish to receive presents, a potluck buffet can be a fabulous way to celebrate. Be sure to organize the food offerings brought by each and every guest in advance, or you'll wind up with fifty trays of cookies. No one needs to make a vast amount of one thing. A dish that feeds eight to ten will supplement a handsome array of samplers. Be sure to take into account how many dishes will need reheating or refrigeration and plan in accordance with the size of your kitchen. You will want to provide all the necessary utensils, glassware, linens, condiments, beverages, etc. as well as a formal wedding cake, if you want one. It may sound like a lot of work, but the end result could be the surprise wedding of the year — an event your guests will talk about for a long time to come!

Chapter 9

Your Bridal Party

"And Pretty Little Maids All in a Row"

By now, you've gathered your best friends and family to act as your bridesmaids and maid or matron of honor. And you've probably vowed, as all brides do, that the bridesmaids' attire will "definitely be something they can wear again." Well, this is a nice gesture. But judging by all the bridesmaids' apparel I've seen over the years, that means these young ladies dine regularly at the Captain's table on the Love Boat.

Unless you select tea-length or shorter skirts, it is nearly impossible to come up with a outfit that can be worn "in real life." So what do you do?

The bridesmaids are traditionally responsible for the cost of their dresses and accessories. You provide their bouquets, as well as overnight accommodations, when necessary. With this in mind, consider the following options:

* ★ When browsing through bridal magazines, be realistic about the heights and figures of your bridesmaids. If anyone is on the heavy side, or very short, you will not want to adorn them in dresses that will detract from their lovelier features. Where do sashes cinch? Avoid off-the-shoulder gowns if someone in your party is "well endowed," or ask her confidentially if she is comfortable in a strapless bra.

* Show your bridesmaids a variety of pictures that appeal to you, quoting the range of prices. You will get a good feel for their budgets without specifically coming out with the question.

* One of the most economical options your bridesmaids have is to rent their outfits (if you are fortunate enough to live in an area where such an offering is available) or to purchase used, sample, or never-completed bridesmaids' attire. Most bridal boutiques carry these now, and so do specialty shops. Unless your bridal party is astronomical in number, you can often find some truly fantastic deals.

Things Happen

What if one of your bridesmaids becomes pregnant? If the timing of your wedding means she is going to "show" too much, she may want to beg out of the proceedings. Try to understand. She might not want to "stand out" in your formal pictures. Instead, you might want to consider asking her if she will do a reading at your ceremony. This offer shows how important she is to you, and will most likely be accepted.

What Does a Bridesmaid Do?

Essentially, not much. They precede you down the aisle and stand witness to your marriage. But they can do much more, if you want them to, such as:

* Ask a bridesmaid to help an usher hand out directions from the church site to the reception. Two people keeps the line moving smoothly.

* If your reception is at a hotel and you have hired a babysitter to watch the children in a guest room, ask a bridesmaid to periodically check on how things are going. The best choice would be someone who also knows that babysitter (if you found a sitter from your neighborhood). But if not, especially in the case of a sitter contracted through the hotel, it's an especially good idea for someone to "drop by" once in a while.

* If you have a table or two of mixed single people, ask any of your more outgoing bridesmaids to visit these tables and promote conversation if things don't seem

to be going well. This particular bridesmaid need only know one person at any given table to get things going. She can introduce herself to the others and ask how they are acquainted with either you or the groom.

* Ask your bridesmaids to dote on your elderly relatives. You and your newly christened husband, as well as both sets of parents, will probably be pulled in all directions, so make sure that grandmothers, great aunts, and other relatives don't feel left out.

What Does the Maid or Matron of Honor Do?

Depending on how close she lives to you, your maid or matron of honor can assist you with any aspect of your wedding that you'd like her to. Typically, she would be in charge of organizing your bridal shower. At the party, she would make a list of your gifts and who gave them to you, just in case tags get misplaced during the display. And if she has good penmanship, your maid or matron of honor can help you with invitations and/or place cards.

Having a problem deciding between your sister and best friend for the post as maid of honor? Choose both! Just keep in mind that you may need an extra usher to create an even number at your head table. (This may depend on whether you choose to seat clergy or a single parent at the head table.) Or, the best man can escort both ladies. A single friend or sister is a maid of honor, and a married one is a matron, but always let a divorced woman decide what she wishes to be called.

The Ushers

Ushers have it easy as far as attire goes. They rent it. The groom and best man should coordinate all fittings, and the best man is in charge of making sure that all tuxedos are returned in good shape to the store within the allotted time. The only exception to this would be when the best man is from out of town. In this case, a reliable usher is elevated to the position of "Keeper of the Clothes."

Is it a problem when some of the ushers don't live in the area? No, especially if you check the franchise chains that rent tuxedos. Ask the sales representative to locate the store nearest to each usher who resides out of town. Then, if you like their prices, let them make arrangements with their sister stores for your "long distance" ushers. But if this does not work out, ask for size chart cards that the ushers would take to a local men's clothing store. A sales clerk there would take and list all appropriate measurements. This is a courtesy that any fine establishment will offer to do. The cards are simply mailed back to your local store, and — *voilà!* — little or no problems. Any out-of-town usher should, however, do his best to have a local fitting the week of your wedding, just to be sure all is well.

What Do the Groomsmen Do?

The best man is in charge of the wedding rings. Together with your maid of honor, the best man signs as witness on your marriage license. If desired, your best man can also act as your spokesman during the reception. If the band is too loud, or the bar has run out of beer, it is generally the best man who seeks out the proper person to remedy the problem. But aside from their "ushering" guests into the ceremony, the groom's attendants seem to have little else to do. They can, however:

* Pass out directions from the church site to the reception.

* Make sure that everyone who will appear in formal pictures is accounted for after the ceremony, and in cars that start! (Don't laugh. I've hosted more than a few weddings where the wedding party had to wait for people who had car problems.)

* Make sure that everyone who is in formal pictures proceeds to the proper picture site. It's a good idea to have these cars travel together.

* At your reception, single ushers could be asked to invite your single female friends to dance. (Who knows what it may lead to!)

* And for receptions that end after dark, ushers might be asked to escort unattended ladies to their cars.

Whatever the case, and whatever they do, gather your most cherished of friends and family and share the special joys of the best day of your life!

Chapter 10

The Beautiful Bride

Choosing the Gown
That's Right for You

hoosing your wedding gown can be one of the most memorable highlights of your life. It can also be one of the most emotionally exhausting ordeals you've ever endured.

Browsing through bridal magazines can almost be a mistake. You see, falling in love with the gown in a full-page ad can spell disaster, for the general rule is: The larger the ad, the larger the price tag. So what can you do?

First, **establish your budget**. This makes your shopping much easier. Second, **ask friends and family for their recommendations of bridal shops.** You will want to visit only the best. And this doesn't necessarily mean the ones who charge the most. This means the ones who have been around awhile. Out of my file of wedding stories comes to mind one in which a bride I worked with found out at the last minute that her boutique went out of business. Just like that! No phone call. No refund. And no dress. She had to rent one. If you have the willpower, visit a few shops without trying anything on. This is the time to be critical. Browse through the dresses in your price range and evaluate the service help. Are they helpful or pushy? Down-to-earth or "snooty"? You must like the shop and its employees. After all, you're going to be together a very long time!

Narrow down the field and return to the shop or shops you liked best for an afternoon or evening of "fun-filled" fittings. Just remember to:

* Wear or bring heels much like you will wear at your wedding.

* Wear a strapless bra if you are interested in trying on gowns with mesh or fine lace around the upper chest and shoulders.

* Sweep up your hair in a simple knot with tendrils on the side, if you think you'll want to have your hair up on your wedding day. This will help you envision the total effect.

* Try not to wear too much makeup, especially base foundation. No matter how careful you are, it can easily smear on the dress.

* Avoid wearing dangling earrings or bracelets that can snag on the delicate material of the gowns.

Try on only dresses that are priced within your budget. It is useless to disappoint yourself. And try on as many different styles as possible. You can't always judge a gown by its appearance on a hanger. When I got married, I went to the boutique with one definite style in mind. The salesperson — who reminded me of a wonderful Italian grandmother — did not disagree with me. She simply brought me some "other" choices as well. No hype. No push. But she had a "favorite" in that bunch. Well, I ended up with that favorite. And it cost me less than what I intended to spend!

Sample gowns are generally made in sizes 8, 10, and 12. So, if you just happen to be out of the "norm," make sure the sales representative assists, by displaying the gown on you to its best advantage.

And for that matter, if you are a perfect size 8, 10, or 12, you just might want to check out the sample gowns on sale. (That's where I got mine!) The deals are fabulous! True, the dresses are most often last year's models. But who, besides you, is going to know that? Don't worry about any makeup stains or wrinkles. The boutique will remove these, and usually at no extra charge. You may get a designer wedding gown for a fraction of the cost!

You'll know the gown of your dreams the very moment you try it on. Hopefully, your mother and/or maid or matron of honor is with you and has brought a camera!

True to the tradition of her time, Scarlett O'Hara in "Gone With the Wind" wore her mother's wedding gown. But with her engagement to Charles Hamilton lasting all of two weeks, Scarlett probably didn't have a choice! Coincidentally, her courtship with husband number two (Frank Kennedy) was also two weeks. And although we don't know for sure, Scarlett probably wore the green velvet dress she made from her mother's curtains, for it was just after the war, and fine clothing was scarce. For her wedding to Rhett Butler, we have no record of what Scarlett wore. But we do know that Rhett went to England for "months" before he returned with Scarlett's engagement ring: a four-carat diamond surrounded by emeralds. With all that time to plan, Scarlett O'Hara Hamilton Kennedy Butler's wedding gown must have really been something!

When you have made your choice, listen carefully to all policies. Know exactly what you are paying for. Will this particular gown require additional articles of clothing, such as full-hoop petticoats or a special brassiere? Does the style of dress require a very formal veil? (These things will strongly affect your budget!) Are alterations included? If not, what are the fees? If hourly rates are being quoted, don't be afraid to ask for the estimated number of hours involved in completing your gown. What kind of deposit is required? Whenever possible, use your credit card. If the boutique does not come through for you as promised, you may have some recourse through your credit card company.

Now if your budget isn't quite up to "boutique," there are **other sources** available for bridal gowns, as well. You can **rent**. (Check your Yellow Pages.) You can read through your local **want ads** for used or never-worn bridal attire. And, if your mother preserved her gown, you can **restore** and/or **alter** hers to fit you. Don't be afraid of saying the style doesn't suit you. Just say it nicely.

You also needn't wear traditional white. In Victorian-style Christmas weddings, often the bride will be in emerald green and the bridesmaids in lush red velvets (or vice versa). I've even seen weddings with the bride in blue, which is true to 18th-century tradition. The choice is yours. And the sky's the limit!

Okay, it's time to be brutally honest with yourself. **Are you really planning to lose weight before your wedding?** If so, inform your salesperson or seamstress. (They're used to hearing it, believe me.) Then lose that weight before your first fitting, and do your best to maintain your desired weight. The problems are all too obvious when you gain or lose more than a few pounds before your final fitting.

Losing weight on your own? That's fine when you have about ten pounds to lose. Just figure on a pound a week, and safely schedule your first fitting around that if time allows.

Want to lose more? Seek out a professional weight control service. They will set up a program for you that gets you where you want to be in a reasonable amount of time. The money is well worth it.

Never, never starve yourself. It doesn't teach you any good habits, and often destroys your health if you do too much of it. And above all, please don't feel under pressure to be someone you're not! After all, your fiancé proposed to you the way you are. The need to trim off a few pounds is normal. But to carve yourself down from a size 12 to a 3 is ridiculous!

Helpful Hints for Hair and Nail Care

Any experimentations with hair color or style changes should be tried at least six months prior to your wedding. If the effect is great, you can repeat it. If a disaster, you have time to repair the damage.

Adding highlights to your own natural color is a subtle but lovely change. The procedure takes approximately two hours, and typically costs three to four times what a standard "color rinse" would. But it lasts far longer (four to six months as compared to an average of four to six weeks for the regular color application). And if you have long, full hair, you may want to consider sweeping it up and adorning it with flowers and/or pearls. This is a breathtaking alternative to wearing a veil.

Whatever the case, visit your hairdresser six months prior to your wedding date. If your normal stylist does not have experience pinning up hair, and that is what you want, have him or her refer you to another stylist in the shop. Bring pictures of styles that intrigue you, or arrive extra early for your consultation appointment so that you'll have time to browse through any design books the salon may have. With six months' advance notice, you can grow out any layering problems that conflict with your chosen bridal style.

You will want to book your appointment for your wedding day six months in advance. Check with the stylist as to how long this appointment will last, and schedule according to your special day's events. If you're getting married on a Sunday, make sure the stylist knows this, and is available to assist you. Because most salons are closed on Sunday, he or she will most likely have to come to your house. Check with your bridesmaids and ask if they might want to have their hair styled as well. Depending on how many will request service, that one stylist might be able to accommodate everyone. (Any bridesmaids who are interested should come in to the salon for a consultation prior to the wedding day.) Each person should get a price quote for the service requested. If the stylist(s) come to your house, please be prepared to pay by cash or check payable to the stylist(s) directly. They are, after all, working on their own time.

Now back to you, the bride. If you are wearing a veil, book a second appointment with that stylist and bring the veil so that he or she can work with it. This appointment should be fairly close to your wedding day so that the design stays fresh in the stylist's mind. Reconfirm all details for your wedding day, and get a list of everything you should be supplying (such as flowers, pearl barrettes, etc.).

Wherever your hair is done — at the salon, your home, or the ceremony site — remember to wear a button-down shirt so that you can change into your wedding gown easily. And of course, if your hair is being done at the salon, **bring your veil!** It is much better for the stylist to pin it on for you. Someone else may not set the crown of your veil in the right place and unintentionally dismantle all of the stylist's hard work.

Some of us have long, beautiful natural nails. And some have lovely acrylic nails. And then there are those of us who type, do dishes, or garden . . . and have lengthy lists of excuses as to why our nails look awful.

For those of us with very short nails who need help, a French manicure is a lovely finishing touch. If you are dealing with a full-service salon, book your nail appointment prior to having your hair done on your wedding day. This way, any accidental smudges can be repaired on the spot. But if you're getting married on a Sunday, and the manicurist doesn't make house calls, have your nails done on Saturday. Just give yourself ample "drying" time at the salon.

Deciding What Makeup Is Best

You probably apply your own makeup every day, and do quite well with it. But what the eye sees and the camera reports are two different things. Visit the cosmetic department of any fine department store, or a specialty makeup boutique, if one is available in your area. Each offers highly trained technicians who will spend an hour or so with you, applying different eyeshadows, liners, foundation, blusher, and lipsticks.

How do you pick the right technician? Wait for the one whose own personal makeup you admire the most. (Of course, if there are any male technicians, observe their presentation and personality.) What should you tell them? First of all, your own preference. Do you generally wear little or no makeup by choice? Do you want something slightly exotic, or just a simple enhancement of your own features? You will also want to tell your technician whether your wedding will be during the day or evening. Do you plan on making regular visits to the local tanning salon before the big day? This figures a great deal in your choice of base foundations. And last, but not least, select a lipstick that stands up well to all the kissing you'll have to face on your wedding day.

Afraid you won't be able to apply this makeup in the same way? Is your maid or matron of honor skillful? Or, perhaps one of the bridesmaids? Then bring that person, as well as a camera, with you. Take close-up pictures — one with your eyes open, and one with eyelids closed, but the eyebrows lifted so that the shadow design will show clearly.

No one in the bridal party and/or in your house confident enough to play makeup artist? Call your hair salon. If there aren't any stylists who excel in makeup application, they certainly can refer someone to you!

There are those who are going to tell you that buying "name" cosmetics is a terrible waste of money. Well, they are right to a certain degree. Some technicians do push those "top notch" items while the everyday brands are just as good. As a matter of fact, I have a lot of great everyday cosmetics. But for my wedding, I wanted to pamper myself in the make-up department. And I did, somehow, feel "prettier" because of it. I maintain that visiting a technician teaches or refreshes you on photo basics. You'll learn not to line your eyes (makes you look tired) and when less eyeshadow is more. It's up to you. But it's your day — **why not pamper yourself?**

Look in the front rows at any wedding ceremony and you're sure to see the silent but proud moms smiling serenely in their billowing folds of baby-bland pastel chiffons . . .

Why is it only dad who gets to dress to the nines on your wedding day? Moms are special too! Now, I'm not suggesting that your mother make a grand entrance at your wedding, decked out like Elizabeth Taylor in "Cleopatra." Unless you feel overshadowed by the thought, a snazzy cocktail dress would suit a nighttime reception and complement your father's attire as well. Or, a style patterned after your maid or matron of honor's gown would show that mom is definitely a loving part of your very special day. And don't forget your future mother-in-law!

Traditionally, the bride's mother decides whether the moms will wear long or short gowns. But if all is amicable, suggest that they decide together. After all, the best solution is a dress they can wear again someday — that is, if they can get dad to rent that tux one more time!

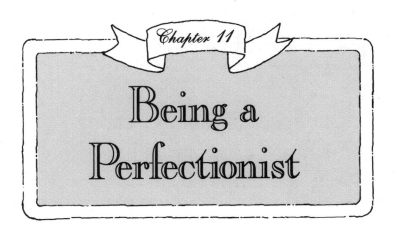

Chapter 11

Being a Perfectionist

The day will come — if it hasn't already — that you realize all the initial groundwork has been laid for your wedding day. At first you're truly amazed, and then perhaps a little depressed. You look at the months and months that lie ahead of you and sigh. Seems like there's nothing left to do, doesn't it?

Wrong. You see, this is where most brides make their first unfortunate mistake. We all rush out there and get the basics done. And then we think, "Oh, I won't have to finalize that until a week or so before the wedding," and we file it all away for later. The problem with "later" is that there will be so much to think about. And the brides who save it all for later are generally the ones who fold under last-minute pressures, and end up wishing the whole thing was over.

Don't be one of these unhappy brides. Get organized for the future now. After all, wouldn't it be a pleasant surprise to actually enjoy your own wedding?

During the Lull

Never put off 'til tomorrow what can be done today. It's a well-worn adage but all too applicable.

The very first step is to create a schedule of all your future activities. Use a calendar or pin-up lists — whatever organizes you best — and list everything you have to do: deposit deadlines, meetings, fittings, important decision-making days, whom to call and at what number. Remind yourself along the way what it is you should be thinking about.

Don't ignore even the tiniest detail. In those last few nerve-racking weeks before your wedding, it is easy to forget even the most obvious of duties.

Here are some other things to be thinking about during those "in between" months.

Special Music Selections
for Your Ceremony and Reception

Ceremony Music: Finalize your selections based on the accompaniment you plan to have. If your musicians do not have a tape for you to listen to, go to your public library and borrow copies of the pieces appropriate for your wedding day. **Reception Music:** Your first dance number is typically an easy decision. But unless you make your band or DJ aware of any other songs you like to hear, the choices will be left to them.

Sometimes it's hard to remember what songs were important to you and your fiancé two or three years ago. And radio is such a fickle medium. Many stations play only the music of the moment. But songs from the past can not only bring happy memories to you, but to many of your wedding guests, as well.

You know those sometimes silly television ads for multi-record or CD collections — the ones that bring back the 50s, 60s, and 70s . . . love songs, rock songs, and disco? Well, I think we can all confess to remembering a song or two from those ads that reminds us of some good time, and we smile. So, why not have a pad of paper and pen by the TV? Whenever one of those ads comes on, jot down any titles that strike you. Don't forget to list the band or vocalist's name whenever possible. Then contact your bandleader or DJ and ask if they can play these numbers. DJs usually have a vast inventory of songs. And if bands have been around awhile, they have dabbled in the top 40s through the years. Having the artists' names will help when the song title alone isn't enough to refresh their memory. Now, if the band doesn't know the song, and it's important for you to hear it, do your best to locate the sheet music and/or the original recording, in ample time for the band to learn it.

While we're on the subject of music — are there any special guests attending your wedding who will be celebrating their wedding anniversary on, or very near, your special day? Then why not present them with a thoughtful gift? Ask your band or DJ to call them to the floor with a rendition of their first dance number! It's easy enough to find out their special song. If they're good friends and didn't get married all that long ago, give them a call. Express some sense of difficulty in choosing your own first dance selection and ask how they came to choose theirs. They'll most likely tell you the title without your even asking!

For older guests and relatives, your undercover work may require some assistance. Contact a friend or family member who may know, or can easily find out for you without causing too much suspicion. And even if your own parents' wedding anniversary is months away, you may wish to honor them with some appropriate song. The same applies to your future in-laws.

Any special birthdays? Have the band sing "Happy Birthday." Will your work friends or college buddies be there? Is there any song that conjures up great memories of the past? You get the idea.

Celebrate your day with song!

Gifts: Yours and Others

Register with the store or stores of your choice as early as possible. Be specific about the items you'd like to have. China is easy. Flatware is simple. But don't just say "blue towels." Between all the famous-maker companies, there are probably no less than a dozen different shades of blue. And the same goes for table linens. Don't just say "floral." You can easily indicate your preferences by listing the maker's name and pattern code and/or descriptive color. And try to utilize at least one store that is convenient to your out-of-state guests.

Select gifts for your bridesmaids and maid or matron of honor early. Jewelry has always remained a traditional gift, and the best prices can be found directly after Christmas and Valentine's Day. You can also be creative. Knit, sew, or embroider if you have the time and the talent! Remember that not every bridesmaid need receive the same gift. Consider each personality and what it is that bonds you together. Was one particular bridesmaid a dearest friend since childhood? When you were little, did she fall in love with your teddy bear? Then get her a special one all her own. (No one is ever too old for a stuffed animal!) Did another give up her ski weekend to stroll down the aisle with you? Get her a couple of lift passes. And so on. Traditionally, your maid or matron of honor should receive a gift somewhat better than the rest. But with each token so truly custom designed, who could ever place a price tag on gifts of such thought and love?

Whatever the case, select your bridal party gifts early. If you wait until those few short weeks before the wedding, you won't be able to devote individual attention to each offering.

Miscellaneous Supplies

If you didn't receive your guest book and pen, cake knife, and wine toast glasses as gifts, you will need to get these items now (unless of course they are included in your wedding package plan). The prices vary greatly from store to store, so shop around. Some bookstores offer the best prices and variety on guest books — (just remember to get a pen!) And discount party supply stores generally can provide you with the rest.

If you choose to have your wedding cake cut up and sent home with the guests, you will have to supply your caterer or reception facility with the necessary napkins, boxes, or bags.

A party supply store is a good source for such an item. You can have napkins printed with your names and wedding date for both your cake and your bar service. Keep in mind that cocktail-size napkins are not large enough for cake slices. Cake bags are not very popular — the frosting sticks too easily to the inside. Boxes, although the easiest form of transport, can mean extra work for you. Cake boxes are sold flat. And very few function facilities are going to offer to set them up for you without charging a fee! So choose accordingly.

Place Cards

Place cards can be as ornate or as simple as you want them to be. Your printer or party supply store can supply you with samples and prices to suit any taste and budget. And although smoking is going out of style, matchbooks can double as place cards and keepsake. Just make sure that anything you have printed includes "Table # ____" because you will not want to write it over and over again, especially on a glossy matchbook cover!

You can also be creative. Check your Yellow Pages for calligraphers. If none is listed, call or visit a local art supply store or art school for recommendations. Then you can get some lovely designer flat cards, have the calligrapher write out each guest's name and table number, and using a small hole-puncher, attach the card with ribbon that matches your bridal party colors. The ribbon can then hold a small keepsake, such as a net wrapping of candies, chocolates or mints. (Just make sure that the candies are individually wrapped.) The only drawback to hiring a calligrapher is that he or she may not be available when you have any last-minute additions or table changes.

Chapter 12

Detailing Your Very Special Day

Your Ceremony

Well in advance of your wedding day, you will want to perfect the details of your wedding vows. Understand from your officiant all the dos and don'ts. May poetry be read? (If so, make sure that your clergy has adequate time to approve your selections.) Would a vocalist be permitted to sing secular music? Get a listing of all the traditional, accepted, and sometimes demanded choices available for readings and music and make your selections early.

Select music that best suits the musician(s) you plan to have. And read your contract carefully. Due to the costly value of musical instruments, some performers reserve the right not to play in severe changes of humidity. If you are hiring a vocalist, he or she should be able to provide you with a list of material they perform best. If you have a different song or two in mind, check with your church for approval first, and then contact the vocalist.

Assign readings. And have "back-up" people ready just in case. The speakers will appreciate the ability to become familiar with their readings in advance.

Your Reception and All its Trimmings

Your Receiving Line

To save time, the best moment to receive your guests is directly after the ceremony. A hundred or so guests will easily flow by in 25 minutes. If you wait until the reception — particularly after everyone has had a drink or two — you can count on it taking roughly 45 minutes per every 125 guests! This can result in a lot of wasted "party" time!

You will have to ask your house of worship if you can conduct your receiving line right after the ceremony. You may be denied your request if a service or another wedding immediately follows yours. The best location for your receiving line would be the front walkway. But if there is not adequate space — or the weather fails you — you can always set yourselves up in the entrance foyer. Ushers could be asked to direct the guests accordingly.

Who is in the receiving line? This is entirely up to you. My suggestion for a perfect gathering would be, in order: your father, your mother, the groom's mother, the groom's father, the best man, the bride and groom, and last but never least, the maid or matron of honor. If the groom's parents are primarily hosting the wedding, they would simply change places with your parents. And of course, if there is any difficulty of divorce with your parents, you will want to alter this accordingly. Definitely include grandparents if they are willing and able. It's a wonderful moment for them.

Including all of the bridesmaids and ushers can be time consuming. Instead, ask a bridesmaid and usher to stand a few feet away from the end of the receiving line and hand out maps to the reception site. (Use more of the bridal party if your guest count is over 200, or if the directions need some explaining.) Other members of the bridal party can be assigned important jobs. Remember the altar flowers (if they're yours to take). Someone can check the pews for forgotten purses, etc. And ushers can make sure that cars are starting and people are safely on their way.

Your Reception

Your banquet coordinator has probably informed you that approximately a month or so before the wedding you should get together and discuss the details of your reception. The timing is right for the most part, for it is only closer to your wedding day that you will know how many guests are coming. But in order to have your day go your way, you will have to do some planning and thinking in advance of this appointment. Don't let such important decisions wait until the last minute when you're so overwhelmed by everything you end up not caring what goes on.

The following is an outline of wedding day events. Now these are only descriptions and suggestions. By reading through this together with your fiancé, you will be better able to finalize your special day when the time comes, fully confident and hassle free!

Your Arrival

The very first thing you will need to let your reception coordinator know is the exact length of your ceremony. Make sure to add time for the receiving line if it is to be held at the ceremony site.

Will the bridal party be pausing en route for pictures at an outdoor location? Let your coordinator know. You also should have contacted your photographer and limousine driver with all the pertinent information.

Next, you will need to let your coordinator know when you expect the bridal party to arrive at the reception. Your on-site host or hostess will want to be on hand to greet you! Will additional formal pictures be taken at the reception site? If so, you will want to settle the following questions:

1. Forty-five minutes to one hour is generally devoted to taking formal portraits. If you are stopping on the way from the church to the reception for pictures, estimate how much additional time, if any, you might wish to have at the reception site for more pictures.

2. If formal pictures are being taken at the reception site, ask if a waiter or waitress will be available to take drink orders in the picture room. Will you be paying for these drinks, or will individuals be responsible for their own charges?

3. If a full hour of pictures is scheduled at the reception site with a receiving line to follow, you may wish to provide your bridal party with a small hors d'oeuvres tray. Select neat, easy-to-eat finger food, such as cheese and crackers and raw vegetables.

If any of your family or friends not in the bridal party have offered to take pictures for you, tell them to come to the picture room with camera ready. A polite professional photographer will always step out of the way after every formal grouping and allow a few moments for others to take pictures.

Your Guests' Arrival

You can't leave your guests stranded during formal pictures. The bar at your reception site should be set to serve guests approximately 15 minutes after the close of your ceremony. The following also applies:

1. Decide how you wish your bar to be handled. Will it be open bar, cash bar, or a combination of both? (That is, for example, open bar for the first hour, then cash.)

2. Will you need hors d'oeuvres? This depends on the time of day, what kind of meal you're serving, and if more than the first hour and a half of the reception is devoted to formal portraits followed by a receiving line. If a full dinner is being served, you will need to provide only about four pieces per person. Decide what offerings intrigue you, and place your order approximately two weeks before the wedding, when your guest count dictates your need.

A lovely hors d'oeuvres idea is a cheese, vegetable, and fruit table centrally placed on the dance floor. This arrangement requires no cumbersome chafing dishes or trays. The food is instead colorfully arrayed on different levels, which are created by placing support bases of various heights under the tablecloth. The effect is like a sumptuous still life oil painting! The table is then moved off the dance floor when it is time to announce the bridal party.

It's a very sad fact, but some dishonest hotels and banquet facilities make money by serving only half the food that has been ordered. And wedding reception hors d'oeuvres are an easy money maker. The reason is simple. Typically, the people who have placed the order — you or your parents — are usually preoccupied in the picture room when hors d'oeuvres are being served and don't notice. But you should. Ask someone who is not in the bridal party to keep an eye on things for you. Make him or her aware of exactly what you have contracted to serve. Keep honest people honest, and have the satisfaction of knowing that what you ordered was actually brought out to your guests.

Guest Comforts

Do any of your guests need special attention? For example, if your function facility has a separate entrance for handicapped guests, be sure to indicate your need for this service. Any dietary problems? Does someone need to bring medication that must be refrigerated? Whatever the case, make sure the facility knows all about it.

Your Announcement
Into the Room

After formal pictures, the bridal party is announced into the room. However, if you prefer to do without the fanfare, a quiet group arrival during the cocktail hour is quite acceptable. When the receiving line has been completed, the bridal party simply walks in procession to its place at the head table.

You may design the seating of the head table in any way that suits you. There are no rules to follow. It is merely suggested that the bride and groom occupy the center seats. You can have parents with you, or seat them at the tables of prominence (numbers one and two). You may also include clergy at the head table, or with your parents. You can have all women on one side with the men on the other, or seat them as couples. Whatever pleases you.

The announcement of the bridal party usually begins with both sets of parents. If this is uncomfortable for anyone because of separation or divorce, alter it accordingly. There are a million suggestions for a million different situations, but I'd like to offer one thought. If your mother has no one to escort her into the room, an usher — particularly one who is a son, relative, or a good family friend — can enter the room with her, and then return to the line and enter once again with a bridesmaid. Just do what is best for everyone involved.

If you have very young children acting as flower girl and ring bearer in your bridal party, and wish to include them in the announcements, you will need to position their "call" in the easiest manner possible. It is recommended that a relative or parent of each child be standing in the function room as a "goal post" (if the dance floor is central to the room's entrance, have that person stand there) and instruct the children to walk towards them. Announcing small children right after the parents is typically best.

The bridesmaids and ushers are next. The easiest way to call them in is by their seating at the head table, working from the outside to the center. But this is also up to you.

Next follows the maid or matron of honor with the best man. And then — take a deep breath — this will probably be the first time you'll hear yourself called "Mr. and Mrs." over a microphone! Your band leader or DJ should have supplied you with a form to fill out for your wedding day information. If you are dealing with a package plan facility, your reception coordinator might do this for you at your appointment to finalize details. Whatever the case, be sure that difficult-to-pronounce names are written out phonetically for the ease of the emcee when announcing the bridal party.

Receiving Line at the Reception

If you were unable or unwilling to conduct your receiving line at the church, now is the best time to have it.

Your on-site coordinator should be on hand to direct the incoming bridal party to where they should stand. Those members of the bridal party not in the receiving line should simply be instructed to walk behind the head table and pause there until the receiving line begins.

The band or DJ is then instructed to announce that the bridal party is ready to receive guests and call up by table number the tables closest to the host of the receiving line, and so on until all tables have gone through. The on-site coordinator will most likely step forward and assist the first table to the receiving line.

As I mentioned, a receiving line that occurs during a reception always takes longer than one held immediately after the ceremony. After a few drinks, guests always seem to want to tell you their firsthand impressions of your wedding. (It's like being at work the morning after a violent thunderstorm. Everyone has a "where they were" story!) If you find anyone lagging, politely interrupt them with a greeting to the person directly behind them and keep the line moving. Every minute of a receiving line during a reception represents one less minute of dancing!

During the receiving line, the best man usually collects all gift envelopes. Provide one of those satin drawstring bags, or some other means of holding these money envelopes. Your on-site coordinator should be on hand to take any large boxed gifts to the gift table, but if he or she is busy with other duties, ask a bridesmaid or usher not involved in the receiving line to do this for you. Any money envelopes found on the gift table should be brought directly to the best man. Don't remove the regular card envelopes from gift boxes, however. You will have difficulty later trying to figure out who sent what!

The Blessing and the Toast

After the receiving line, the bridal party is escorted to the head table. The best man (or whoever was asked to collect them) brings the gift envelopes with him to the head table for safekeeping. Everyone is asked to stand. Your clergy is then asked to give the blessing. Be sure to have a back-up person if your clergy cannot attend. If there is no one in your family or close friends who wishes to speak publicly, your band or DJ can give a general blessing.

Everyone is then asked to remain standing except the bride and groom. The best man then gives his toast, and the meal begins. Before going to your appointment with your coordinator, have a good idea what you would like to have for your toast and your meal.

Once the meal begins, the on-site coordinator should accompany the groom and best man to the safe-deposit box where your gift envelopes will be locked away. Both the best man and groom should sign the authorization lines. The best man generally holds the key, in case more gift envelopes are presented. Each time he makes a deposit to the safe, he will be asked to sign in and out. At the end of the night, the key is given to the groom. Your coordinator will probably warn you that there is only one key. If it is lost, you will have to pay a locksmith's fee to get the box open. So be careful!

Your First Dance

After the first course of your wedding dinner, I suggest that you and the groom come to the floor for your first dance. Try not to wait until the meal is over, because traditionally no one is supposed to get up and dance before the bride and groom do. With this in mind, if you really prefer to wait, or to cancel the ritual altogether, have your band or DJ announce that both of you (by name) invite everyone to the dance floor at any time. Keep in mind that if you and the groom are nervous about dancing alone, the band or DJ can be instructed to call up the rest of the bridal party to join you as early on as you wish! In between courses is the best time to conduct the special events of your reception. During these times, you will have everyone's attention. And it gives people something to do during the clearing and serving of plates.

Parents' Dances

If you are dancing with your father and/or the groom is dancing with his mother, this can be done in between courses. For example, you have your *first dance* after the soup course, and *parents' dances* after the salad course. If the traditional numbers don't appeal to you ("Daddy's Little Girl" for you and your father and "Sunrise Sunset" for the groom and his mother) select songs that hold special meaning for you.

The Dollar Dance

This is an opportunity for your male guests to share the dance floor with the bride for cash (something like a kissing booth at a fair). Each gentleman hands you a bill which you hold between your fingers. It's not so common a custom these days, but really is harmless fun, all the same.

Special Guest Dances

Make note to inform your coordinator of any special anniversary dances or birthdays that you would like the band or DJ to celebrate. If you are dealing with package plan entertainment, your coordinator will need to list this on his or her activities sheet, if you haven't already contacted the band or DJ on your own and confirmed these special request songs!

"The Bride Cuts the Cake"

If the wedding cake is to be served with dessert, you will need to have your cake-cutting ceremony just after the main course.

Don't worry if you despise the silly song and all the fanfare. If you like, the band or DJ can announce that anyone who wishes to take pictures of the bride and groom cutting the cake can proceed to the cake table. Then your on-site coordinator and professional photographer will quietly guide you through the steps. No song. No smooshing cake in each other's faces. (Or be a sly one and smoosh anyway!)

Awarding Table Centerpieces

Unless you have someone special in mind to whom you'd like to give the centerpiece at each table, your band or DJ can create a "game" competition for the centerpieces. The most common asks one person at each table to take out a dollar bill. That dollar bill is then passed around the table until the music stops. Then, the band announces that the person holding the dollar keeps it, and the original donor of the bill gets the centerpiece. But if many of your guests have been to weddings, they'll know this one.

Be creative. You can even somewhat "pre-arrange" your winners if you wish. Let's say you'd really love your grandmother to have a centerpiece. Have the band announce that the oldest person at her table number wins the centerpiece (if that is the case). Go by the birthday closest to your wedding day. Have a "sing the next line of the song" contest. This is accomplished by the lead singer going from table to table with a wireless microphone. He or she sings a song up to a certain point and then surprises one of the guests at each table with the chance to go on with the song. Be crafty. For example, do you and "the girls" from work have a bowling night? Award that centerpiece to "the worst bowler at table number ten." In other words, make it fun and involve your guests!

The Bouquet and Garter Toss

If you and your groom intend to leave the reception before the majority of guests, you will need to coordinate the last hour of your reception to include the bouquet and garter toss, enough time for you and your groom to change into your "going away" clothes, sit for some formal portraits, and return to the ballroom for your final dance.

But if you are not leaving the reception before the guests, the bouquet and garter toss can be done at any time. Often it is best to just mingle, circulate, and dance after dinner. The bouquet and garter toss is always more fun towards the end of the evening, anyway. Just don't wait too long. You will want to have this fun while the band or DJ and photographer are still there, not to mention a good number of guests!)

Keeping the Hall Late

A five-hour wedding reception can fly by like five minutes. With all the planning and hopes you've had for this day, why not keep the party going?

The band or other musicians can be booked for additional hours, or a DJ can be brought in for a change of pace. Another possible suggestion would be to book a DJ or singer with karaoke hook-up. Karaoke can be great fun when everyone has had a drink or two and is willing to "give it a try." You will, however, want dance music, too. Of course, any arrangement for entertainment should have been made well in advance of that day!

Get all the formal pictures you need before the photographer leaves. Most brides don't feel like surrendering their wedding gowns just yet, so the final shot in your going-away clothes may not seem all that important to you.

Holding the hall for extra hours gives you another option I have not as yet pointed out. If between you and the groom, you have a lot of casual friends you just couldn't afford to invite for the full meal, etc., you can now invite them for a special evening celebration of your marriage.

You may want to consider holding an open bar for any or all of these additional hours. But don't, if you are concerned about the people who have been drinking for the last 5 hours who might be staying. One possibility is to give your newly arriving guests "drink tickets." But for those new guests, as well as those who will be staying and may need some help sobering up, some delectables would be a good idea.

Suggestions for Late-Night Food and Beverage Service

A deli buffet is a great idea. People can make a sandwich, a salad, or a meat platter — whatever they wish. Sweet tables with coffee service are also nice. Depending on your taste and budget, arrange an offering that best suits your needs.

Your Last Dance

This is when your guests form a circle around the bride and groom, and smile and cry as you join together for the last dance of the evening. A good guide to selecting what should be your first dance and what should be your last is to consider how they will be performed. If a band opens your reception, pick the song they can easily do. (In other words, it takes a terribly talented vocalist to match the depth and dynamics of a Whitney Houston or a Mariah Carey!) And if a DJ closes for you, he or she has the true artist's rendition of your special song, complete with full orchestration. But of course, there's no reason not to repeat the same song for your first and last dance, especially when it's one that means so very much to you.

Aside from the events outlined here, you may also have some wonderful ideas based on the traditions of your family's heritage. By all means, incorporate these family traditions, but be sure to let the proper service professionals at your wedding know well in advance what they will need to do.

Yes, this is the time to plan, to design, and to dream. The days ahead will be happier ones if you meet them fully organized!

Chapter 13

Getting It All Together

Finalizing Your Reception Plans

he months have flown. And now you can easily chant the very number of weeks, days, hours, and minutes 'til the time you say, "I do!"

Six to eight weeks prior to the big day, your calendar should spell out every duty left to do. Look now for days that seem overloaded with tasks and distribute them more evenly. Don't try to do the impossible.

During one of your final appointments with your reception coordinator, he or she will be giving you some room diagrams and seating charts to work with. Your coordinator will need these listings in order to double-check your place cards and guest count. And your on-site host or hostess will need a copy just in case you have any last-minute deletions or changes on your wedding day.

If you have a choice in the numbering of your guest tables, I would suggest placing all even numbers on one side of the room with odd numbers on the other. The lower the number, the closer that table is to the head table. And yes, you can skip number 13 if you so desire.

During this appointment with your coordinator, you should also verify:

> ★ Are all outside service aspects provided by the facility confirmed, such as the limo, band, photographer, bakery, and florist? If you have not spoken directly with the limo company, band leader (or DJ) or photographer

yet (package plan only), make note of this to your coordinator. The limo company may not need to speak with you until a week or so before the wedding as they will just be reconfirming your address and time, but you will still want to be sure that everything is fine and going as scheduled!

* Verify all service aspects that you will be providing. Make sure that your reception site has contacts and phone numbers. The reason is simple. If on your wedding day your cake is not showing up on time, your on-site coordinator can call the bakery direct and hopefully avoid upsetting you at home. Without a phone number, your wedding day host or hostess may be forced to wait until your arrival to do something about it. And by then, it will most likely be too late.

* Reconfirm linen colors.

* Thoroughly go over all the scheduled events of your wedding reception. Has adequate time been allotted to every detail? If your coordinator is making up a printed schedule, ask for a copy when it is ready. (A sample schedule appears at the end of this chapter, should you want to do your own.)

* Know when you have to finalize your dinner and hors d'oeuvres menus. When is the exact or "guaranteed" guest count due for meals? Arrange your appointment for final payment. This is typically done three business days before the wedding. List everything that you will have to bring with you, such as place cards, table listings, guest book, keepsakes, etc. And make your coordinator aware of any item you do not wish to bring early, such as a valuable cake top. Inform him or her of when and how such items will arrive.

* Reconfirm all prices. Have your coordinator run another tape list of costs based on the guest count you expect to have. **In your count include all the guests that have informed you they are coming to your wedding, as well as those that have not yet replied.** Make sure that all your deposits have been accounted for. Your correct balance due will be calculated when your guest counts and menus have been finalized.

★ If you are dealing with a hotel, reconfirm all your overnight reservations before leaving.

Coping with Room Diagrams and Seating Charts

Don't wait until the last minute to contact guests who haven't yet replied to your invitation. A few days past the response date is fine for making phone calls. After all, you don't want to have to rearrange your seating charts every time a late reply comes in. The earlier you get your table arrangements done, the earlier you can enjoy all the parties and attention a bride receives in those last few weeks before the wedding.

Dealing with seating arrangements can be a very stressful time in a bride's life. And this can be especially true when both sets of parents are contributing financially to your wedding. Why? Because no one wants their guests "seated out in left field." (Yes, that's what they'll call it.) So what can you do?

To begin with, your parents — along with the friends or family of their choice — should be seated at table number one. The groom's parents and selected company occupy table number two. The only exception to this is when the groom's parents have paid for the wedding. Then they are seated at table number one.

Traditionally, the closer the family member or friend, the closer they are seated to the head table. Dividing the room in half may help your particular dilemma. If your parents are at table one, number all the rest of the tables on that side of the room with odd numbers and assign those to your parents. Thus, the groom's parents at table two get all the even numbered tables on their side of the room. Each party is then welcome to seat their tables as they wish. (Just give them a deadline or you'll never have it done on time!) You and your groom should be allotted one third of the tables by taking the "middle" section from each side of the room. Just remember to seat older guests far from the band to avoid the loud music. And count any wheelchair arrival as taking up two "chair" spaces for extra comfort.

If you are personally writing out your own place cards, try not to do too many in one sitting or your exhaustion will show in your penmanship.

Make sure that your guests' names are easy to read. Watch out for name duplication, which typically occurs when a father and son with the same name are invited. In such a case, add *Sr., Jr., I, II, III,* or whatever is appropriate. When you're not sure of the title, add the spouse or date with each, (such as: "Robert and Betty Harrison" on one and "Robert and Sue Harrison" on the other). When a guest has informed you of an escort's name, it is a nice gesture to write out that person's name. Just remember that the initial invitee's name goes first on the card, regardless of alphabetical order.

Putting It All in Writing

As soon as you can finalize menus and schedules with your reception site, do so. Then you can put the events of your day down on paper and see for yourself if there is anything else left to be done. And by giving your banquet facility a copy of your list, you just might notify them of a minor detail or two they unintentionally overlooked.

The following sample schedule assumes you are providing every service aspect of the wedding reception except food and beverages. Alter it to meets your own needs. (For example, next to **Band**, type in the name of the band and indicate "provided through facility.")

The Hamilton-Cartwright Reception
Saturday, May 21st, 1994
  Contact: Erica Hamilton (bride)
    16 Laurel Drive
    Belmont Hills, MA 01234
    Home phone: (617) 555-0201
    Business phone: (617) 555-2223

Ceremony: St. Mary's Church of West Belmont
  4:15 p.m.–6 p.m. — Includes receiving line

Reception: The Wedgewood Ballroom at the
  Belmont Plaza
6 p.m.–closing — 1001 Cambridge Way
  Belmont Hills, MA 01266
  (617) 555-1776
Contact: Mike Gallagher
Total number of guests, including bridal party: 187

Room Setup Notes: White tablecloths with light-blue napkins.

Accessories Setup: See Sales Office for guest book and
pen, toast glasses, and cake knife (**provided by bride**),
as well as for room diagram, place cards, and keepsake
matchbooks. Please set one matchbook per place setting
with remainder placed in large brandy snifter on the bar.

Flowers: Will be delivered on **May 21st**
between **4:30–5 p.m.**
by: **Fantasy Florists**
66 Main Street
Belmont Hills, MA
(617) 555-5200
Karen or Cathy
**Please have guest tables prepared with tablecloths
and chairs.** The florists have to arrange keepsake ornaments to match the number of chairs per table.

Cake: To be delivered at **5 p.m.**
by **Heavenly Creations**
129 Main Street
Belmont Hills, MA
(617) 555-4783
Trisha or Diane
Please have cake table skirted and ready.

Band: Set-up: **5 p.m.**
Hours: 6–10 p.m.
Once in a Lifetime
Contact: Chris Wade
Phone: (508) 555-3750

Limo: Fleetwood Productions
55 North Highland Ave.
Belmont Hills, MA
Contact: Jeffrey Allen
Phone: (617) 555-8901

Photographer: Lasting Impressions Studio
of Photography
101 Main Street
Belmont Hills, MA
Contact: Matthew or Melanie
On-site photographer: Sandy Pierson
Phone: (617) 555-9922

DJ: Setup at 9 p.m.
Hours: 10 p.m.–12:45 a.m.
Butchie Clarke
Phone: (617) 555-1983

Guest Arrival: 6 p.m.

Bridal Party Arrival: 6:45 p.m.

Please Note: There will be one handicapped guest
arriving via the back entrance, as arranged with Mike
in the sales office.

Also Note: The bridal party will be stopping at the
Prescott Gardens for formal pictures, weather permitting.
If inclement weather, formal portraits will be
taken in the picture room at the Belmont Plaza from
approximately 6:15–7:15 p.m.

Hors d'oeuvres: 6 p.m. (Ballroom)
Cheese, Fruit, and Vegetable Table
2 Trays Stuffed Mushroom Caps
2 Iced Shrimp Cocktail Bowls
2 Trays Rumaki

Bar: 6 p.m.–Closing
Open Bar: 6 p.m. until close of dinner
Cash Bar: Remainder of evening
Please Note: Nonalcoholic beer requested for
the groom.

Picture Room:
> **Formal Portraits: 6:45–7:15 p.m.** (6:15–7:15 p.m. if weather inclement)
> Please have waitstaff on hand to take drink orders, on an open-bar basis.

Hors d'oeuvres in Picture Room: 1 small cheese, vegetable, and fruit tray for 16 people.

Announcement of Bridal Party: 7:15 p.m.
> The parents of the bride: John and Marcia Hamilton
> The parents of the groom: Franklin and Lucy Cartwright
> The flower girl and ring bearer: Courtney Wallace and Jarrett Corcoran
> The bridesmaids and ushers:
>> Margie Brigham and Ted Carlton
>> Debbie Myers and Skip Jones
>> Jennifer Travers and Al Columbo
> The maid of honor and best man: Helen Farnsworth and Charles E. Gardner
> The bride and groom: Mr. and Mrs. Thomas Cartwright (Erica and Tom)

Blessing: To be said by Father O'Hara. (In the absence of clergy, please call on the bride's uncle, Mr. Paul Hamilton.)

Toast: Champagne. (Please offer ginger ale and fruit juice alternatives to all tables.)

Toast to be given by the best man, Charles E. Gardner (college buddy of the groom).

Dinner: To begin approximately 7:30 p.m.
Fresh fruit cup
Sorbet
Hearts of palm salad
Boneless breast of chicken with cranberry sage stuffing
Honey-glazed carrots
Duchess potatoes
Wedding cake served with mocha swirl ice cream
Coffee, tea, decaf
Plus two (2) hamburger plates for flower girl and ring bearer, both seated at Table #4.

Please Note: The band and photographer are cordially invited by Erica and Tom to enjoy a meal at their convenience.

First Dance: Directly after first course.
"Vision of Love" by Mariah Carey
Please ask bridal party to join in after first chorus

Parents' Dances: Directly after the salad course.
The bride: Erica will dance with her father, Mr. John Hamilton, to "Unforgettable" (duo version by Natalie Cole and Nat King Cole)
The groom: Tom will dance with his mother, Lucy Cartwright, to "Sunrise, Sunset"

Cake-Cutting: After main course.

Traditional Song:
Staff Note: After cake-cutting, please place all tier pillars and separators in the Heavenly Creations box provided.
Jennifer Travers, a bridesmaid, will collect these at the end of the evening to return to bakery. She will also be responsible for collecting the top tier and cake top.

Special Requests for the Band:
>Friends of the bride and groom: Robin and Chris Benoit, are celebrating their tenth anniversary on May 24th. Please call them up with "Could I Have This Dance" by Ann Murray.
>
>Please sing "Happy Birthday" to Miss Faith Gordon who is 26 today.

Centerpieces: To be awarded in the following manner:
>Each guest will find a heart-shaped ornament facing his or her chair. The ribbon attached to each ornament is hidden under the ivy ring surrounding the centerpiece. Ask each guest to pull the ornament out from under the ivy. The one with the gold ribbon wins the centerpiece.

Bouquet and Garter Toss:
>Prior to band's departure at 10 p.m. — **Traditional**

DJ: sets up approximately 9 p.m.
>Begins at 10 p.m. when band concludes. DJ has a listing of requested music.

Additional Food Service: 10:30 p.m.
>Deli buffet with assorted sodas, coffee, tea, and decaf.

Last Dance: Approximately 11:45 p.m.
>The bride and groom will dance to: "Why Can't This Night Go on Forever," by Journey.
>
>Then go to: "The Time of My Life" from *Dirty Dancing* for all remaining guests to join in.

Note: The bride and groom are not changing into going-away clothes.

Letting Friends and Family Help

Good Ideas for Wedding Day Volunteers!

. Since the moment you announced your engagement, you were probably besieged with offers to "do whatever needs doing." This is wonderful. By all means, you should allow people to lend a hand. After all, you can't do everything yourself. But be sure that the person making the offer is reliable! Many a friend or family member will talk a good game, but will they actually go to bat for you?

The following are ideas of what can be done by volunteers outside of your bridal party. I have already covered some, but will repeat them here for good measure:

* **Obtain a housesitter** for your parents' home and your home, for the hours of your wedding and reception. This unfortunately means someone who cannot attend your wedding. The groom's parents may also wish to consider doing the same, as a safeguard against burglary.

* Will you need **babysitting service** for the children of out-of-town family or friends? If your parents are willing, the children can be watched at their home, alleviating the need for a separate housesitter.

* Finalize all volunteers to take **pictures** and **videotapes** of your wedding day. Find out what film you need for each person and buy adequate quantities. Assign one person to **collect all film**. Whether or not you have that person drop it off for development is up to you. If your honeymoon plans keep you away longer than three weeks or so, that person should notify the shop of your estimated pick-up date. Otherwise, the shop may consider your photos abandoned material.

* Select "guardians" for your **open bar** and **hors d'oeuvres**. These volunteers should not be a part of the bridal party. Give your hors d'oeuvres guardian a list of what you have ordered. Your beverage guardian should place himself or herself at the bar. While maintaining an easy flow of conversation with their fellow guests, your bar guardian should keep one eye on the bartenders. Too much over pouring? If an adding machine or cash register is being used to calculate prices, is one price entry being made per drink? Are top-of-the-line brands being used only when requested? Now,

should a problem with either service occur, the guardian should approach a waiter or waitress and ask for the reception coordinator or manager, in order to solve the problem quietly and efficiently.

* Are **delivery** people needed on your wedding day? For example, are you providing a cake top that you didn't wish to leave with the banquet office three days before your wedding? Were your ceremony programs inadvertently left at home on rehearsal night? A volunteer driver comes in handy in situations such as these.

* And, speaking of **drivers**, do you have to go to your final hair appointment alone? Ask someone to bring you. You're going to be nervous and excited, which affects your driving skills. Also you're going to have a huge veil on your head which only makes your peripheral vision even worse. So, take along a calm friend who knows everything you are supposed to bring with you (such as pins, barrettes, combs, flowers, **your veil**, etc.)!

* **Pack a large cosmetic bag** (preferably one with a strap or a handle), with any or all of the following:

> fresh mascara
> your wedding day eyeshadow
> blush and powder
> your lipstick shade
> a small container of hair spray
> brush or comb
> hair pins, barrettes, or combs
> small makeup mirror
> nail file
> a spare pair of your wedding day hosiery
> safety pins of various sizes
> quick-hold glue for heels
> eye drops
> aspirin
> breath mints

Include any other items of personal preference, such as your favorite perfume, and ask that a female friend not in the bridal party pick up this bag at your home or your parents' home on her way to the church. This volunteer should be invited to the picture room, in case you should need anything.

* If you have provided your own wedding cake, chances are the **support columns** and **dividers** need to be **returned to the bakery**. Any volunteers?

* Did you supply your own **bar service**? All the **unopened bottles** will either have to go **back to the store for refund**, or brought to your parents' house, or wherever you dictate. Is someone willing to do this for you?

* Any **specialty items** that you **rented** (such as a champagne fountains, chairs, etc.) will also need to be **cleaned and returned**. If you are dealing with several rented items, it is best, not to mention thoughtful, to ask a "team" to help. After all, many hands make light work!

* The **tuxedos** must be returned. Of course, between the ushers and the best man, someone in the wedding party should be in charge of this function. But, if for any reason, no one is, seek out someone who can do this for you. Just keep in mind that if the rental store is not open on Sunday (or more important, if your wedding is on a Sunday), that volunteer must be able to return them by the time limit indicated on Monday!

* The same request applies if you **rented your gown.**

* **Airport transportation** may be necessary for you and the groom. Of course, you can always rent a limo and go in style. (Just make sure, however, that someone is on hand to pick you up when you get home!)

Chapter 14

With Many Thanks

Gratuities, Expected and Otherwise

With so many people dedicating their time to making your wedding day a memorable one, it is customary to want to express your gratitude in some way. But how much and when? That is the question!

Thanking your friends is always easy. You seem to know just what to do for the person who watched your house, or ran your errands, or even just gave you a shoulder to cry on! But when it comes to thanking people in the service industry, we are never sure when we've given too much or, worse yet, too little. The following represents all the possible facets of your perfect day, complete with suggested gratuities. Of course, only impeccable service need be rewarded above and beyond the norm, so "respond" accordingly!

* **Your church and/or clergy:** In most instances, a requested "donation" has already been asked of you. But if this is not the case, ask your church's secretary what might be appropriate. And always present your clergy (and his or her spouse, when applicable), with an invitation to your reception.

* **Your limo driver:** Unless the gratuity is already included, a standard tip would be 10%–15% of the full service price. Of course, if your driver was less than courteous, don't bother! And, in such an unfortunate

case, be sure to call the company at some point, and express your displeasure to the manager. The company really should know.

* **Your banquet sales representative:** Was he or she extremely helpful and courteous? Did he or she stay past normal office hours on more than one occasion to meet with you? Were you given assistance with creative ideas and/or budgeting problems? One of the nicest gestures you can make is to write a letter to the facility's general manager in praise of this person. Then send a separate thank-you card to your sales rep. You might also considering letting him or her know that you would willingly act as a reference for any future bride. Just be sure to note that you will call about any inquiry yourself, therefore keeping your phone number private.

* **Your reception coordinator:** If your banquet sales rep not only assisted with your plans, but went on to be your wedding day host or hostess as well, you may wish to do a little more than I mentioned above. A special desk memento would be nice. Or, if you conversed on a personal level during your planning sessions, you may know of something more meaningful to him or her. A gift certificate for a favorite restaurant in town? A music box? You needn't spend a lot. It's the gesture of your appreciation that counts.

If a separate coordinator worked with you on your wedding day, a cash gratuity is always nice if that person was attentive, courteous, and personable beyond your expectations. (In other words, was he or she just doing a job, or were you made to feel incredibly special?) Did your coordinator see to the comforts of your guests as well, making sure that everyone was pleased with the food, etc.? Did your day go as you planned it because of this very special person? (That is, were minor problems handled quietly, efficiently, and to your satisfaction?) There is no guideline or percentage to consider when tipping such a person, but somewhere in the range of twenty to twenty-five dollars is quite acceptable.

* **The serving staff:** Banquet servers have a guaranteed percentage of the gratuity you have already paid. But in many facilities, it doesn't always chalk up to 20%. Was your head waiter or waitress extremely attentive to the bridal party's needs? Then multiply the number

of guests the head waiter or waitress was responsible for serving, and multiply that figure by two. (For example 18 x 2 = $36.00.) And if the serving staff in general acted above and beyond the call of graciousness, give the head waiter or waitress $10.00–$15.00 per server and ask that he or she distribute it with your thanks and appreciation.

* **The bartender(s)** will generally be tipped well by your guests. But if you find that they have gone out of their way to be helpful you may wish to present them with $10.00–$15.00 cash as a thank-you for the extra service. (For example, have they brought your drink orders to the head table, themselves? Have they carried drinks to the tables for ladies? Did they assist the serving staff by pouring coffee at dinner time?)

* **Valets and coatroom attendants:** If such people worked a part of your special day, their gratuities should have been amply covered by your guests.

* **Entertainment:** Providing your band or DJ with a meal shows your appreciation for their efforts in making your day a special one. But if you'd like to take it a step further, you could offer to buy them a drink or two.

* **Photographer and/or videographer:** Aside from a complimentary meal and a drink or two from your bar, I would suggest making a cash gratuity when your photographer or videographer agrees to stay later than he or she was contracted for without charging you an additional fee. Figure roughly $20.00 per extra hour.

* **Your florist and baker** typically do not expect to be tipped for their services. But if you felt their efforts deserve recognition, be sure to write letters of praise to each shop.

Once again, these gratuity figures are merely suggestions. After all, good service is to be expected! Only excellent service need be rewarded.

Here's the wedding day "tip" my husband clued me in on, and I now pass it along to you — never give your room key to a grinning usher. . . .

My husband Terry and his merry band of college friends all participated in each others weddings. Being the kind of good buddies they are, each wedded couple received a loving gift from the gang — a completely booby-trapped honeymoon suite.

How does it happen? Typically, the couples most destined for trouble are staying at the hotel where their reception is being held. A seemingly innocent usher comes up to the bride and says that the groom needs the room key, and voila, you've just set yourself up for a night you may soon wish to forget. Yes, you may have imagined your wedding night as an evening of unequaled bliss. But are you ready for short-sheeted beds, greased toilet seats, a 3:00 a.m. wake-up call, and coffee grinds in the shower head?

In all seriousness, you should alert the front desk that no one is to know that you are staying at the hotel. Where I worked, our favorite trick was to pretend to give in and confess that the newlyweds were staying at one of the name hotels at the airport. It may result in your car being sabotaged, but better that than your wedding night privacy.

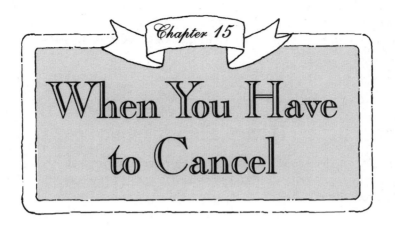

Postponing Your Wedding Due to the Loss of a Loved One

When a death in the family obliges you to postpone your wedding, contact your coordinator as soon as possible. The death of a loved one is a devastating blow, particularly when the passing is a sudden one. When you have lost a mother, a father, a brother or a sister so close to your scheduled wedding date, it is understandable that you may feel you can't go on as planned. In such an unfortunate circumstance, enlist the aid of your bridal party in phoning all your guests. A future date can be announced when you and everyone else concerned are ready to proceed.

Try to realize despite your distress that it may be impossible to move any or all of your deposit money to another date. You will feel angry and frustrated. No one is denying that. But things happen, and business is business. Just make the best of the situation. Enlist the help of your maid or matron of honor, or any of the bridesmaids, and make sure that everyone you are contracted with has been made aware of the change.

In the case of a grandparent, or anyone who is terminally ill at the time of your engagement, it is best to determine in advance what you might wish to do if that person leaves you before your wedding date. Many times this individual will tell you personally to go on with your wedding plans. But there are other people to consider, as well. For example, if it was your mother's mother who passed away, please allow your mother time to evaluate what all this means to her. Each situation is different. And each requires patience and tender loving care.

When You and Your Fiancé Have Called It Quits

Every couple has a tiff or two before the wedding. With all the fuss and planning and excitement and expenses, it's almost expected. But if you can see through the smoke of emotional stress and sense danger in your future, take a long, hard look at things and talk to each other until there is no talking left to do.

You may find (with a surprising sense of relief) that you are better off apart.

Then what happens? Contact your coordinator and all the other professional service people that you are contracted with for your wedding. (If you can't handle it, ask your maid or matron of honor, or some other trusted, well-spoken friend or family member, to do it for you.) Expect to lose all your deposit funds. If you and your "ex" can communicate like adults, you may wish to split the burden equally. For example, if you or your family put down all the deposit money, your "ex" should reimburse the proper person or persons for half the total.

Look into the "recall" notices available to you through your local printer if you have the time for printing and mailing. If not, gather your bridal party and start calling your guests. Determine what you want said. Don't be embarrassed to let people know that the wedding is off due to mutual consent. Let the knowledge that you are saving yourself from a future of hurt and pain be your shield. Return all wedding gifts. You might want to include a brief note of thanks for the donor's concern and understanding. Assure them that you are doing just fine. And then get on with your life.

But what if your fiancé wants to break things off for no apparent reason? This is one of the most emotionally difficult ordeals you will ever have to face in your life. And it can be worse when you didn't see it coming.

Some men are just afraid of marriage. Although this may, in some cases, be a good reason not to get married, it is no excuse for being rude, and certainly not a good excuse for cancelling a wedding that has already been planned. And your fiancé is even more of a coward if he waits until the last minute to let you know.

Everyone reacts to shock and pain differently. But if I may, I would like to point out something I've seen from experience. The ladies in your wedding party will undoubtedly feel almost as shocked as you do. But they will not know what to say to you until you indicate that it is okay to talk about it. Their silence is only out of respect for your feelings. As soon as you are ready, gather them up and go out together. It will most likely be a therapeutic evening for you. Complain. Laugh. Cry. It's the beginning of recovery.

From this side of the page, I can't tell you if the marriage is worth fighting for. Only you know for sure. But never let your pride be your sole warrior (although sometimes that's easier said than done). If the trust has gone out of your relationship, you have nothing to build on, so don't try. When a man cannot give you one good solid reason why he has decided against marrying you, there is no communication. And trust and communication are fundamental to a lifetime of happiness between two people. If it is you who solely and truly feels that the wedding should not go on, know your reasons, state them frankly and clearly, and face the consequences of your decision like an adult. It is only fair.

As I mentioned, you, or someone close to you, should contact all the service people or industries involved with your wedding. If your decision to split has occurred early on, you may be able to recover some of your deposit funds. Given enough notice, your banquet hall, band, photographer, etc. may very easily replace your booking. And should this happen, it is not unreasonable to expect some if not almost all of your money back. (It's fair to lose a small percentage of your money towards a service fee.) One way or the other, it doesn't hurt to ask.

If recall notices can safely be sent to your guests, do so. If it was your fiancé's sole decision to end the engagement, request from either him or his family full payment for printing and postage, as well as any deposit funds you could not recover. If you are met with opposition, let it go. It's not worth making yourself sick.

If lack of time necessitates phone calls, once again decide who will do the calling and what should be said. Return all gifts and include that brief note, if you can. Assure the ones who love you that you will be fine. Because you will!

For some brides who have to cancel their weddings, it's just a sad fact that no matter what you say or do, you can't get your deposits back. So, what do you do?

If you're up to it, have a party! Why not? The banquet room is going to be empty during the hours you have booked it for, and that band or DJ is going to sit idle. So, why not make the most of it? Here's one idea for a party I personally arranged for a few of the "nearly brides" I've worked with.

Get all your bridesmaids and closest friends together and estimate how many friends and family you could invite to a dance social. Then visit your banquet sales representative and see how your deposit money can best be utilized towards such a party. Don't be afraid to negotiate details such as ridiculously high room rentals. The sales rep will realize that any potential food and bar activity is better than the room sitting dark for the night. I would recommend arranging for hors d'oeuvres that suit a large group in the mood for dancing and moderate drinking. Estimate three to four pieces per person of such items as cheese and crackers, veggie trays, or chicken fingers. A cash bar (one where the guests pay for their own drinks) would be fine. The room should have seating for one-half your anticipated crowd. Once you have the estimated costs, ask your guests for a "cover charge" that will help recoup some or all of your funds. But best of all, you are having fun with friends and family on a night you shouldn't be alone.

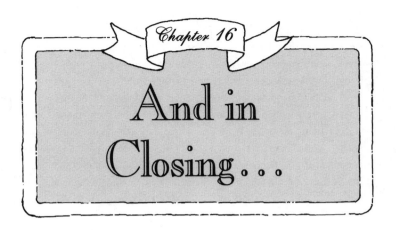

Chapter 16

And in Closing...

Expect Something to Go Wrong

I know what you're thinking. How can this book go on and on about how to prepare for and organize a perfect wedding and then mention the need to expect impending disaster? You've dreamed of this day. You planned for it in exacting detail, to the point that every moment runs through your mind like an Oscar-winning movie. So, with all your notes, your memos, and your endless instruction sheets, how can a blessed thing go wrong?

As Rod Serling opened every episode of the *Twilight Zone*, . . . here is your special day, "submitted for your approval."

> You wake up on your wedding day with a stress blister on your mouth. It's raining. Four guests have called to cancel, but one couple has left word that they have to bring their six kids. The hair salon just called — your stylist is out sick. Your mother is crying. You throw up your cereal. It's still raining. The flower girl's mother is on the phone — the sweet little child has smeared peanut butter all over her $200 designer dress and refuses to wear anything but her "Barney the dinosaur" nightshirt. A bridesmaid shows up on your doorstep — she broke up with her boyfriend last night, who just happens to be her bridal party partner. Can you rearrange the couples, please, oh, please? Your mother's still cry-

ing. The dog was just sprayed by a skunk. Your little brother says you're ugly. Now *you're* crying. Did you just hear thunder? You spill your coffee every time the phone rings. One of the ushers is on the phone — his dress shoes squeak; can he wear sneakers? Your mother manages to dry her tears and find you a hairstylist. She's your Great Aunt Millie who hasn't practiced her trade since Elvis cut his first record. It's still raining. Another bridesmaid calls — she has an abscessed tooth, and the only time her dentist can see her is two hours before the wedding — but don't worry, she'll be there. You rearrange the bridal party a second time. Lightning strikes and the dog dashes under your bed, dragging your wedding veil with him. The lights go out. It's *still* raining. Your father is bathing the dog in tomato juice. The rest of your bridesmaids show up. The maid of honor will be there soon — one of the girls saw her car being towed on the interstate. The best man calls — he can't find the groom. Aunt Millie shows up with a tiger-striped drawstring bag full of sponge rollers. It's pouring out. Finally, the maid of honor arrives. She walked six blocks in the rain, holding her dress over her head. But relax — your little brother just put the dress in the dryer. You throw up for what you hope is the last time, and get ready. Luckily, the maid of honor fits in your old prom gown. The photographer arrives. At least he has his camera. You line up for pictures. The dog runs in and shakes all over everyone. It's definitely time to go. At least the limo driver has an umbrella — you know because he accidentally poked you in the eye with it. You get to the church. You start down the aisle. Where is the groom? Oh, there he is! Guess what — he fainted . . .

Okay, okay, so no bride has ever experienced a wedding day disaster such as this. But in my many years of wedding planning, these kinds of mishaps have really occurred. It is important to realize that things will happen beyond your control! Now, I'm not referring to gross negligence. That is totally inexcusable. I'm referring to the little mishaps that come and go without too much fuss, like a broken heel, or a forgotten garter. Expect it, conquer it, and laugh. No small problem is ever going to destroy your day.

But let's pretend that your reception coordinator comes to you with a real problem. Don't scream, fuss, fume, or faint. Allow him or her to explain how the facility is going to make amends. And if the solution is acceptable, let it simply blow over.

And what if it isn't acceptable? What if the facility is definitely not coming through with something as promised, and you rationally know that the mistake shouldn't have happened. Now, I know it sounds difficult, but do the best you can with the situation. When you get back from your honeymoon, you can bring your complaints to the executive manager of the facility. And whatever happens, don't let it ruin the rest of your day!

Whatever happens on your wedding day (and may it be as minor as a brief rain shower, which, by the way, is good luck!) always remember that you have the strength of family, the devotion of friends, and the love of a special someone "from this day forward"!

You will be a beautiful bride. You will have a beautiful day. There is no doubt in my mind.

My best to you both in your future together as husband and wife. May you share good health, prosperity, and happiness all the days of your lives!

Index